Celtic
Symbols

Celtic
Symbols

UNLOCK ANCIENT WISDOM AND CONNECT
WITH THE SPIRIT OF THE LAND

Joules Taylor

CICO BOOKS
LONDON NEW YORK

This edition published in 2025 by CICO Books
An imprint of Ryland Peters & Small Ltd
20–21 Jockey's Fields   1452 Davis Bugg Road
London WC1R 4BW   Warrenton, NC 27589

www.rylandpeters.com

10 9 8 7 6 5 4 3 2 1

First published in 2008 as
The Book of Celtic Symbols

A CIP catalog record for this book is
available from the Library of Congress
and the British Library.

ISBN: 978-1-80065-410-5

Printed in China

Illustrations: Emma Garner and Ken Taylor
Designer: David Fordham
Editors: Richard Emerson and Marion Paull

Assistant Editor: Danielle Rawlings
Senior designer: Emily Breen
Art director: Sally Powell
Creative director: Leslie Harrington
Head of production: Patricia Harrington
Publishing manager: Carmel Edmonds

AUTHOR'S NOTE

The author makes no claims to the infallibility of
the information offered in this book. Many of the
features of the Celtic culture blend together, over
time, across tribes, and across countries; the
names and functions of deities overlap,
intermingle or diverge depending on the
perceptions of their devotees or the shape of
the land itself. The paucity of the information
available does not make the job any easier,
either. The Romans, who tried to force their
culture on the Celts at the point of a sword, and
later the Christians, who tried to usurp the native
culture with the tools of repression and guilt,
make attempts at reconstruction harder, as their
records are obviously biased.

I have used the most reliable sources I could
find, extrapolated from what is known, and
tried to keep conjecture to what is feasible.
Nevertheless, some of what is written here is
speculative, drawn from the spirit rather than the
records of this proud and sophisticated people.
I trust that I have presented them in the way they
would have wished.

The information and practices detailed in this
book are in no way intended to replace genuine
medical treatment. If you are in any
doubt about any aspect of your physical or
mental health, see a medical professional.

Contents

Introduction
Who Were the Celts?

Our image of the Celtic people has been colored by legend and poetry, the beautiful artwork they left behind, archaeological evidence, and the writings of Roman historians. Although they left almost no written records, their influence is widely felt even today, and their descendants still live in the last fastnesses of the Celtic lands—Eire, Wales, Brittany, Scotland, Cornwall, and the Isle of Man.

So who were they? Their language indicates that as a people they originated on or around the steppes of Central Asia, gradually moving westwards during the second millennium BCE. At the height of Celtic civilization, their lands included most of Europe, most of the British Isles, and some areas of the Middle East and Central Asia. They did not have any form of centralized government or unified political system, and weren't interested in empire building. If they had been, the world would be a very different place today.

We know from historical records and archaeological evidence that they were a tall, strong, mostly fair-haired race, with blue or gray eyes, who used bold color and pattern in clothing and adornment. A dynamic—not to say, fierce—people, they must have been frightening to their less bellicose neighbors and were certainly a source of some awe to the culture that had the most impact upon them, the Roman Empire. The Romans, who, of course, eventually conquered the Celts, wrote about them in a less than flattering light—history is written by the victors in any combat. In addition, the Romans were probably still bitter about the Celtic invaders forcing them to surrender the city of Rome in 387 BCE. Even so, there is a sense of unwilling admiration in the words of the historians.

The Celts were superb horsemen, and absolutely fearless in battle. They believed that a hero's death in combat was the highest honor a warrior could attain, guaranteeing him—or her—a particularly comfortable place in the afterlife and a happy rebirth, probably into a chieftain's family. Women were as capable in battle as men. In fact, the Roman author Ammianus Marcellinus says that if a Celtic woman were to come forward to help her husband in a fight, no one, not even a whole troop of invaders, could stand against them.

The place of women in Celtic society was extraordinarily advanced for the time. They could rule tribes, take part in political life, become warriors and Druids, Bards and healers, choose and divorce their husbands at will—it's possible that they may have been able to take more than one husband at a time—and were surprisingly sexually liberated. Cassius Dio reports that the wife of the Caledonian chieftain Argentocoxus, when rebuked for her loose morals by Julia Domna the Roman Emperor's wife, retorted, "We carry out the demands of nature in a far better way than do you Roman women. We consort openly with the best men, while you let yourselves be degraded in secret by the most contemptible." (Admittedly the Caledonian Britons were Picts rather than Celts, but we have no reason to assume that sexual practices were different between the two peoples, given the similarity of other historical records of Celtic culture and society.)

Much of the Celts' culture and cultural practices were condemned by the Romans, particularly their system of sacrifice, perhaps most notably the burning of criminals and the occasional captive in the "wicker man" (a roughly human-shaped structure woven of willow branches). The Celts used sacrifice to appease their gods, in whom they believed implicitly, and, in the main, the victims were those who had harmed society. The Romans described these practices as "barbaric," although it should be pointed out that around this time they were sending their own captives and criminals, unarmed, to be slaughtered by armed, trained warriors or wild animals in the arena for the pleasure of the viewing populace, or hanging them on crosses to die a slow, agonizing death.

Celtic Society

The Celts' social structure was three-tiered. At the top were the intellectual elite, the Druids, who were the law-givers and judges. They included the two other Druidic disciplines: the Bards—the artists and musicians who sang the tales and the histories of the Celtic people, and the Vates—the priests and seers. Below them were the kings, chiefs, and their "courts," mainly comprising warriors and their spouses, and favored nobles. At the bottom, much as usual, were the people who actually kept society running—the farmers, hunters, herdsmen, metal-workers, artisans, builders, and the families of common folk. The Celts generally lived in small family or tribal agricultural communities rather than cities, although the existence of hillforts shows that, when necessary for defense, the communities would band together for safety.

The Druids taught a doctrine of rebirth, that after death the spirit traveled to Annwn, the Otherworld, to rest and recover before being reincarnated. Whether all people were reborn or just the upper classes isn't wholly clear, but for our purposes let's assume that it was the right of all Celts to come back to earth in another guise. The Celts considered the land to be a goddess, their Great Mother, filled with mystery and peopled by gods and goddesses in the springs, rivers, wells, and caves, in the hills and trees. Their lives moved in accordance with the natural rhythms of the world around them. Underscoring their forceful temperament was a deep reverence for the land, for their deities, and the creatures with which they shared their lives.

But most of all, there was a harmony to the shape of their existence, an understanding that to survive and succeed, one must live attuned to the world in which one has been born, accepting its blessings as well as its misfortunes.

For instance, in a world with no other artificial light than candles, lamps, and firelight, wakefulness and sleep were governed to a large extent by the rising and setting of the sun and moon, and the lengths of day and night.

The Celtic day started at sunset, not midnight as in the current tradition. We still hold to this for some festivals—for instance Samhain (Hallowe'en) starts at sunset and continues until the following morning.

The Celts and Their Symbols

To the Celt, everything in life was symbolic. The Druids read the future in the movement of the stars and planets, in dreams, in the flights of birds, in the running of hares, and in the way blood spurted from a sacrificial victim. Tools, jewelry, and dwellings were circular, echoing and reverencing the curves and rounded lines of nature, plants, the moon, and the safety of the womb. The Celts have been portrayed as primitive worshippers of animals and rocks, whereas in fact their beliefs were closer to a pantheistic view of the universe, where everything breathing or inanimate partakes of the divine, and to give respect and reverence to all things in the world is to respect and reverence the gods, the essence of life itself. It's important, when considering Celtic culture, to bear in mind that for them, the entire world was sacred.

Chapter 1

The Celtic Year

The Celts lived in remarkable harmony with the natural cycles of light and dark, and the changing seasons were marked with festivals. The demands of modern life make compliance with natural rhythms of light and dark difficult, but to connect with the Celtic spirit, and achieve a measure of balance, it is a good idea to make the effort to celebrate at least some of these festivals. All festival dates in this cahpter apply to the Northern Hemisphere—the Celts were a Northern culture. They are also presented as being fixed, although in reality the Celts marked time by the moon, so the modern date would vary slightly from year to year.

It has been suggested that each festival lasted three days, or possibly even three weeks. For our purposes, we'll assume that the Celts were very aware of how much their survival relied on the results of their labor, and that for most people the festival lasted just one night, with the possible exception of Yule.

Dark Year, Light Year

The year could be simply divided into Light, or Bright, Year—from Beltain (May 1) to Samhain (November 1)—and Dark Year—Samhain to Beltain. The Light Year is roughly equivalent to summer, the Dark Year to winter. Most of the work of the community took place during the Light Year, while the Dark Year was a time for surviving the harshness of the cold months.

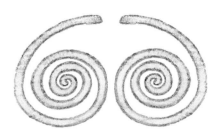

DOUBLE SPIRAL

The double spiral symbolizes balance, the two halves of the year, representing the sun increasing in warmth and brightness during Light Year and decreasing during the Dark Year.

The Fourfold Year

A more complex way of dividing the year is into the four seasons of Spring, Summer, Fall, and Winter. As always in nature, everything flows. There are no sharply dividing lines where one season becomes another. However, the year can be divided into four in two different ways, using the quarter days or the cross-quarter days.

Traditionally, the quarter days were the Solstices and the Equinoxes—the longest and shortest nights and the two days in the year when the length of day and night was equal.

The Spring Equinox, usually March 20, is generally considered to be the feast of Eostre (or Ostara), the goddess of the spring and new growth. Hares and eggs are her symbols, remembered today in the Easter Rabbit and Easter eggs.

The original name for the Autumn Equinox remains undiscovered. Neo-pagans have named it Mabon, although the association of the Divine Youth with the cooling weather, shorter days, and the bounty of the harvest seems misplaced. Modron (the all-providing Mother Goddess) or Rosmerta (the "Good Provider") would be far more appropriate.

Yule and Midsummer mark the Solstices—usually December 22 and June 21 respectively, although the dates can vary by a day or two from year to year. The Midsummer Solstice has no well-known name associated with it, although Litha has been suggested (the name comes from the writings of the Venerable Bede and refers to the Anglo-Saxon names for the months of June and July).

The cross-quarter days fall between the quarter days, and comprise the ancient Celtic festivals of Imbolc (February 1), Beltain (May Day, the first day of spring), Lughnasadh (August 1), and Samhain (November 1). These are the Fire Festivals, celebrations of human life and its connection to the earth—and the Otherworld, in the case of Beltain and Samhain.

THE FOUR-SPOKED SOLAR WHEEL

The four-spoked solar wheel shows the sun dividing the year into four seasons. This also symbolizes Mabon, the Divine Child.

THE EIGHT-SPOKED SOLAR WHEEL

The most comprehensive way to celebrate the year's cycle is to combine the quarter days and cross-quarter days into a year marked by eight festivals. The eight-spoked, or doubled, solar wheel is a very ancient symbol and appears in many cultures, but its meaning as an image of the ever-cycling year is consistent across the world.

The Festivals

SAMHAIN

"End of Summer" sunset October 30 to sunset November 1
*Morrigan and Daghda are the Guides associated with Samhain
(pronounced "SOW-in" or "SAH-wen")*

This was the start of the Celtic Dark Year, the Celtic New Year. On this night the boundaries between the mortal world and Annwn, the Otherworld realm of spirits and deities, grew thin enough for humans and Otherworldly beings to pass between them. It could be a dangerous time. Strangers abroad on this night might be gods in disguise, or malicious or beneficent spirits. It would not be wise to offend them, just in case they could bless or harm us. From this arose the modern custom of "trick or treat." Originally, hospitality would be offered to strangers in the form of shelter, food, and drink, to ensure that they would not curse the household and its family.

Samhain marks the final harvest, and was the time for assessing how much food would be needed to last the winter. It's quite likely that the Druids, as the final authority and with their years of experience, had a hand in this. Any weak or sickly animals were slaughtered for a feast or for smoking, salting, and storing to supplement winter provisions.

Samhain also represented the culmination of the apple harvest, although the apples would probably have been smaller and rather less sweet than modern varieties—the bitter crab apple may have been more frequently used by the general populace, and made more palatable by being sweetened with honey or birch sap, which is sweet like maple sap and may be tapped for the same purpose. The fruit forms a five-pointed star if cut horizontally, usually considered to be symbolic of the human being these days. The shape certainly had a great deal of meaning to the Celts, as it appears on many Celtic coins, often

CELTIC
COIN WITH
HORSE
AND
FIVE-
POINTED
STAR

underneath the image of a horse. Since horses were revered in Celtic culture, it's probably safe to assume that the five-pointed star symbolized wealth or treasure of some kind, although not necessarily earthly.

The festival was celebrated with large bonfires, originally "bonefires"—the bones of slaughtered animals may have been thrown into them as an offering to the gods for their bounty throughout the year, and as a plea for blessings for the coming season. Fire is a small piece of the sun on earth, lending its light, warmth, and power to the community. For luck and good health, animals were driven between two fires as they were brought down from the fields to be sheltered for the winter.

Sweeping through the house from front to back with an old-fashioned broom or besom was said to sweep all the stale matters of the preceding year into the past and leave the dwelling clean and ready for good things in the future. If you have the time and energy, a thorough "Samhain-clean" of your home serves the same purpose.

Samhain is a traditional time for divination. Peeling the skin from an apple in one long strip, throwing it over your shoulder and seeing what letter it resembles when it lands is a fairly modern tradition. The letter is supposed to give you the first letter of your future spouse's name. Bobbing for apples floating in a barrel is an old tradition. The first person to catch an apple was believed to be the next person to marry. Gazing into a mirror by candlelight may also prove enlightening—spirits may use the mirror's reflective power to appear behind you as misty forms, passing messages from the Otherworld.

To commemorate the ancient fire festival, invite family and close friends to share a candlelit "feast"—pork, or boar if it's available, bread (see page 74), and apples are ideal—to be eaten after sunset. Keep apples, toffee apples, or little sweet muffins ready for "trick or treaters"—far more appropriate than candies, although the recipients might not appreciate them so much—and treat any callers on this night with wary respect. They may be spirits in disguise.

Of course, anyone brave enough—and with legal and safe access to such a thing—could spend the night on or near an ancient burial mound. These mounds were believed to be gateways between the worlds, which could open at Samhain and Beltain. It would be unwise to try to follow any beings back to the Otherworld though. Stories tell of days there being equal to years here, and the charm of the place tempting the unwary mortal to stay until all they know in the human world has passed away...

YULE

The Winter Solstice, around December 22

The longest night of the year was always greeted with a feast, song, dance, and much drinking. This may have been, in very ancient times, a way to tempt the sun back up to see what was happening, ensuring that it would continue to rise and set and bring life to the world for another year. Gradually, it became a celebration of the sun's return, a festival of thankfulness that the cycle of the seasons would carry on through another year. There is some evidence that Yule-tide lasted for 12 days (13 nights) rather than just from sunset to sunset, and given the significance of the occasion, this might well have been so. At the darkest time of the year, the community's agricultural work was curtailed, and keeping spirits up with song and tale-telling, if not continual feasting (after all, the foodstores had to last until the earth was fruitful again) would seem to be a pragmatic thing to do.

Evergreen plants were all that grew at this time of year, and so came to be revered as a symbol that life could survive the winter. Holly, with its prickly leaves and cheerful red berries, represented protection from malicious influences, and was used to decorate walls and doors. Mistletoe was a sacred plant and may have been distributed to each family by the Druids to hang in their dwellings as a protective talisman. The Druids regarded mistletoe berries as the semen of the sun, or of the tree on which it grows, and kissing underneath a sprig of it, adapted from a Norse custom, was associated with fertility. Burning a yule log was also probably a Norse tradition. The log, chosen especially for its slow-burning qualities, was expected to last for at least 12 hours as a symbolic replacement for the heat and light of the sun.

Other than remembering the original reason for the celebration—the return of the life-giving sun—and starting the celebrations on the true date of the Solstice, commemorating Yule doesn't involve any special preparations.

IMBOLC

The festival of returning spring, sunset January 31—February 1, associated with Briggida.

The name Imbolc comes from the Irish for "in the womb" and traditionally refers to pregnant sheep. It was originally associated with the onset of lactation in ewes, a sign that they would soon give birth to spring lambs. Sheep didn't have as high a standing in Celtic culture as horses or cattle, but they were valued for their meat and their fleece, which was used to make clothing.

The festival marked the start of the farming season. The first signs of new green plant growth appeared as the warmer and longer days woke the earth from her winter sleep. It was a time of preparation for the coming year—making sure that all the tools were repaired and ready for use, clothing was in good order, and that all was ready for the community's work. Fields were ploughed in readiness for the first sowings, new candles were made, and firewood stocks were replenished. These days it's known as spring cleaning!

Few flowers bloom at this time of year. The snowdrop is the best-known, often peeking through the snow and bringing gladness and joy at renewed growth to those who see it. The Celts would have known the snowdrop, native to the UK and widely spread throughout northern Europe. It is a sturdy little flower, despite its delicate appearance, and its deceptive fragility is emblematic of life overcoming all difficulties.

To commemorate Imbolc, first make sure any lingering little jobs and chores are completed, all the things that have been put off over the winter. Then celebrate by going for a walk, in the country or in a park. Use the time to search for early signs of spring, such as buds on bushes and trees, stirring insects, and birds building nests. Focus on your senses—be aware of how the world smells and sounds as well as what you can see.

EOSTRE

Spring Equinox, usually March 20

The Spring Equinox marked the beginning of spring proper. The first shoots of the newly sown crops would now be just showing in the fields, the leaves on tree and bush would be opening, and flower buds appearing. Early fledglings would have left the nest, the parent birds would be busy feeding the next brood. On British hillsides, hares (not rabbits, they are non-native and were brought over by the Normans) were leaping and cavorting in their courtship rituals, and their conspicuous displays led to them being intimately associated with the festival as a symbol of energy and passion.

While Easter is purportedly a solemn Christian occasion, the Easter eggs and Easter rabbits that appear everywhere in modern times are a powerful testament to, and reminder of, the origin of the festival—of joy in life and happy fertility.

Celebrate Eostre with loved ones, preferably in the open air. It's a good time to make plans for the coming year in any aspect of life.

BELTAIN

May Day, Bel's festival, sunset April 30 to sunset May 1

Dancing around the Maypole is a traditional way to celebrate a very old festival. Beltain—Bel's Fire, the return of the heat of the summer sun and the start of the Light Year—symbolizes fertility at its most basic, a lusty, earthy joy in living. The maypole itself is a very obvious symbol of male fertility and potency.

The festival celebrates the union of Cernunnos—the Lord of the Dance, the Lord of Nature—with the Great Mother to make the world fruitful and healthy. This continues today with the choosing of a May Queen and her consort, which originally symbolized the marriage of the man chosen by the Druids as most fit to be king, to the land, in the form of the goddess.

As with all Celtic fire festivals, Beltain included the lighting of bonfires, and possibly leading livestock between them for Bel's blessing. Leaping over the Beltain bonfire was thought to foster fertility and bring good fortune, although it's not something to be undertaken lightly, in case of injury!

As at Samhain, boundaries with the Otherworld grew thin at Beltain. The festival was lighter but it was still unwise to offend any strangers or spirits that might be abroad, although they were more likely to join in the festivities than make demands.

Celebrate by partying until dawn. Women should wash their faces in the morning dew. Beltain dew is traditionally the best of the year for making women beautiful, in spirit if not in body, especially if it has been gathered from an oak or hawthorn tree.

SUMMER SOLSTICE

Sometimes called Litha, usually June 21

This is the shortest night of the year, and the point at which the nights began to lengthen again on the slide down to the Dark Year. Traditionally, herbs and flowers gathered at this time had the greatest efficacy and healing qualities, having absorbed the light and power of the sun during its climb to its highest point.

The festival marks a brief pause in the year. This is a time to draw breath and rest from your labors before the important work of harvesting begins, and making sure there's enough food to sustain the community through the Dark Year. Even though the hottest days of summer are often yet to come, there's nevertheless the slightest touch of sadness about the midsummer solstice, an instinctive knowledge that the nights will now grow longer.

Stay up all night to welcome the sun at dawn. Greet its rising with a mug of mead (see page 73), remembering to spill a few drops on to the earth as a token of thanks for all that she has provided throughout the year.

LUGHNASADH

Sunset July 31 to sunset August 1, associated with Lugh
(pronounced "loo-nah-sah")

Lughnasadh marks the start of the harvest and the beginning of the intensely busy and vital preparations for the coming Dark Year. Irish tradition says Lugh organized the festival in memory of his foster-mother. Single-handedly, she cleared the plains of Ireland in preparation for the establishment of farms and the beginning of agriculture, dying of exhaustion as she completed the task. At this festival, communities gathered for trade and family reunions, and horse-racing and feats of strength took place, along with unarmed combat to confirm and reassert warrior status within the tribes.

These days many craft fayres take place around this time. Take the opportunity to visit one, in the country if you can, keeping in mind the work that has gone into providing the produce you see around you.

AUTUMN EQUINOX

Usually September 23, herein named Modron

The Autumn Equinox signals the end of the grain and vegetable harvest.
By now the crops should be stored, and plans for surviving the coming months
be well under way. Animals are being rounded up to be herded back to the
safety of the village surrounds. The last game animals are being hunted
in forest and moor, the last fish of the fall are being salted or smoked for
storage, and wood is being gathered and chopped for the fires that
will burn through the winter.

Now is the time to take stock of all that has been accomplished,
and list objectives still to be attained, mentally adjusting to working
towards them next year.

Keep in Touch With Nature

City living often precludes owning a garden or easy access to the countryside,
yet to gain an insight into the Celtic attitude toward nature, it's important to
have as much contact as possible with greenery and living things. Spend time
in the nearest park, especially if you can take a break from work there. Use the
time to stretch your senses. Touch leaves, bark, and petals, enjoy the scent of
flowers and sap, listen to birdsong and the wind. Eat lunch in the open air and
share scraps with the wild birds. If it's raining, take shelter under the trees. In
winter, appreciate the luxury of being able to return somewhere warm after
being cold. Study the clouds, learn to anticipate the weather—it's as important
to us today as it was to the Celts, albeit for different reasons.

If you have no garden, grow a plant on a windowsill. Herbs are an excellent choice, attractive both to look at and to smell. They add flavor to dishes and have a beneficial effect on health. Thyme and parsley are tasty condiments. Yarrow smells pleasant and used in moderation adds a peppery flavor to salads. Vervain is considered a magically protective plant rather than being used in cooking. Meadowsweet fills the air with the scent of vanilla. Strewn on the floors of ancient dwellings, it was used as an air freshener and pest-repellent. For color and interest, try wild European poppies (representing the Mother Goddess) or Lunaria (commonly known as Honesty), a pretty, intriguingly scented plant with silver full-moon-shaped seed pods, symbolic of Arianrhod. Leave the window open when you can, to encourage insects to pollinate the plants.

There is an intimate joy in growing things, and seeing them flourish, no matter for how brief a time. It creates an important symbolic connection to the land from which we spring and on which we depend.

Chapter 2

Celtic Guides and Their Symbols

At birth each and every one of us has vast potential to be anyone and anything we desire. As we grow, however, much of that potential is lost under layers of experience as we learn, or are told, what is and is not considered *possible*.

Our parents may close off important avenues of expression. Being told we can't sing at the age of eight may dampen our confidence ever to try again, for example. Not being allowed construction toys or dance lessons may stunt an embryonic talent in those fields. This is not usually malicious—we are all products of the time and culture into which we're born—but it may have a lasting effect on our lives. In our education we may be thwarted by the system, peer-pressure, or our own laziness.

Later, we may decide to overcome those mental blocks and draw upon the potential lurking in the depths of our psyche, waiting to be summoned. The Celtic Guides here represent all aspects of the human spirit: they are archetypes, embodying qualities we lack or need to strengthen. Learning about them, feeling them resonate within us, developing their attributes, and exploring how best to express their intimate meaning, can release a flood of untapped potential to enlighten and empower our lives.

The Great Mother

The Great Mother embodied the land of the Celts. She was the greatest
of deities, revered as the mother of all things. Without her there would be
no life. She is a triple goddess, representing the three essential stages of a
woman's life—Briggida the Maiden, Modron the Mother, and the Old Wise
Woman. She is usually depicted as three often-identical women, accompanied
by infants, fruit, and bread, symbolizing her fertility. The varying aspects of the
Great Mother are interchangeable, and will appeal to different devotees at
different times or for different purposes.

BRIGGIDA THE MAIDEN

Briggida may be regarded as a maiden, but she is no fragile, submissive virgin to be cosseted. Celtic women were strong and independent, and viewed their goddesses likewise. Briggida (Bride, Bright) is creative, a civilized and civilizing goddess, skilled in fine metalwork. Her attributes are light, inspiration, energy, and the fertility that was the entitlement of all goddesses. Nurturing and caring, she embodies the youthful zeal of the young woman just entering adulthood, rejoicing in her forthcoming fruitfulness—of body and mind.

New beginnings, conception, inception, and creativity are all Briggida's province. Her feast is Imbolc.

MODRON THE MOTHER

Modron is a somewhat shadowy figure, less knowable than other aspects of the Great Mother. Modron symbolizes the fertile earth, and more primal characteristics of the mother figure. She is fiercely protective of her children, prepared to do what is necessary—even kill—to safeguard them. She may be called upon when her children are in danger or faced with seemingly insurmountable obstacles. Mabon the Divine Youth is her son (see page 36).

Modron's attributes are fulfilment, power, strength, and stamina.

THE OLD WISE WOMAN

Often, unkindly, called the Crone, the Wise Woman represents the last stage of womanhood—age and the wisdom gathered from the uniquely female experience of life. Generally tolerant and kindly, she shares her knowledge freely, and welcomes those who seek wisdom—but she's no fool, and can be frightening and remorseless when angered.

Wisdom, rest, sleep, and death are in the Old Wise Woman's charge.

A THREE-FOLD NATURE

These three aspects of the Mother Goddess are not necessarily independent or separate. They represent the whole course of life, from beginning to end, the process of change, of growing and developing, learning, maturing, and passing on what has been learned. Thus these three act as guides for everyone, in all walks of life.

The triple spiral of the triskele symbolizes the Great Mother's three-fold nature. The three spirals are separate yet interconnected. They resemble a puzzle, and in that lies much of their significance. Life itself can be seen as a maze, with choices and dead ends, wrong turns and sudden revelations. The wisdom and knowledge gained along the way will help you to make correct decisions, take the right paths for you, and at the end comes the satisfaction of having successfully negotiated the maze.

Daghdha

Daghdha was the "Good" god. "Good" here means being proficient at everything he did rather than implying superior moral qualities. Where the triple goddess symbolized the Great Mother, the Daghdha represented the Father. He was a gigantic and extremely powerful figure. He owned a staff or club that could kill nine men with a single blow from one end, and restore the slain to life using the other end. His cauldron produced food in limitless quantities, no matter how many required feeding. He was a god of knowledge, venerated by the Druids as their main deity.

However, he was not without humor. He did not mind a joke at his own expense, and was sometimes portrayed as a buffoon, dressed in a short tunic that revealed buttocks and genitals. He teaches that knowledge should be tempered with humor, that there must be a balance of opposites in life.

Daghdha's symbol is the strong solidity of the simple square shield knot (pictured on his shield above). Its symmetrical pattern acts as a balance to the swirling complexity of the Great Mother's triskele, and emphasizes the need for equanimity in dealing with others.

Mabon, the Divine Child

Mabon is the Divine Child who becomes the Divine Youth. He is the eternally young Celtic god of music and harmony, liberation and unity. He was kidnapped from his mother when he was three days old, and held in a dungeon in Gloucester, England, until freed by the heroes Kai and Gwrhyr. (In the Welsh tradition Mabon was detained in Annwn, the Otherworld, and his liberator was Culhwch.) Mabon represents imprisonment of the spirit and release from captivity, and symbolizes rebirth or reincarnation in his re-emergence from Annwn.

Mabon is always charming, eloquent and musically skilled—a fine and trustworthy companion. He acts as mediator between the gods and humanity, when needed.

Mabon's attributes are intercession, negotiation, persuasion, and the ability to soothe anger. His symbol is the four-spoked solar wheel, representing the cycles of life, death, and rebirth, the turning of the year and the treasures that the changing seasons bring. The image combines the fluid, curling lines of the triskele and the solidity of Daghdha's shield knot, demonstrating Mabon's versatility and adaptability.

Arianrhod

In Welsh mythology Arianrhod was the daughter of the Welsh mother goddess Dôn, the sister of the magician Gwydion, and the mother of the twins Dylan Eil Don (Dylan—"great tide"—son of the wave [see page 46]) and Lleu Llaw Gyffes (Lleu—"fair" or "lion"—skilful hand, for his killing of a wren with a single thrown stone [see page 47]). The children were born when she was magically challenged to prove her virginity. The fact that she fled in embarrassment immediately afterward, leaving Dylan to escape to the sea and Gwydion to pick up and care for Lleu for the first few years of his life, has been taken by some to indicate that the twins were the result of incest between Arianrhod and her brother Gwydion.

What else we know of Arianrhod has to be deduced from her legends. That she was extremely powerful is apparent. She was able to stop her son Lleu being named. Thus she prevent him from living a "real" life, until she permitted it. She also stopped him bearing arms, unless she provided them, and prevented him from marrying a human woman, simply by decreeing it so. He was only able to overcome the *tynghedau* (curses) by the trickery of his uncle Gwydion. Her other son was a sea spirit who vanished into the waves soon after he was born, never to set foot on land again. This fact, together with the meaning of her name—"silver wheel"—implies that she was a moon goddess, possibly a pre-Celtic one, controlling the tides of the sea. The connection between the moon's course along the line of the ecliptic and hence the Zodiacal belt, and influence over the fates of humans, is subtle. Yet it would have been noted by the Druids, whose astronomical and occult knowledge was extensive. The constellation Corona Borealis (the Northern Crown) is known as Caer Arianrhod, "Arianrhod's Castle," to the Welsh, reinforcing the celestial connection.

On an emotional and spiritual level, Arianrhod symbolizes the hidden forces in our lives, the complex web of human emotions and relationships. She has been likened to a weaver, working behind the scenes to shape the lives and destinies of others. She is a cool and distant deity, far above the matters of the earth yet connected to them by the power she wields over the sea. As such she has a better overview of the course of human life than earthbound mortals.

Arianrhod's attributes are control, a deep understanding of things hidden to human sight, and silent, intuitive guidance. Her symbol is a silver moon, or, to represent her weaver aspect, a spider on a web.

Belenus/Lugh

Belenus, the Shining One, was a solar god, associated with heat, light, and general good health. Sometimes known simply as "Bel," he protected the sheep and cattle that were essential to the Celtic way of life. His Irish counterpart was many-skilled Lugh, the deity presiding over travel, craftwork, and trade. Between them they covered the growing season, from the first shoots of spring marked by Beltain, named in Bel's honor, to the ripening grain and harvest celebrated at Lughnasadh, Lugh's feast.

In a farming culture, so heavily reliant on the weather, reverence to the sun was naturally important. Beltain was celebrated with dancing and bonfires, while Lughnasadh became a time for fayres, social occasions, and get-togethers.

Belenus/Lugh symbolize growth and health, development and communication, celebration and fertility. Like the Great Mother, they are all-embracing, but lack her immediacy and intimacy. They govern groups of people rather than individuals. Their symbol is the eight-spoked solar wheel.

Arawn

Arawn was the Lord of Annwn, the Otherworld, a place of great beauty and tranquility where souls went to rest after death. Arawn always dressed in a gray cloak. He was generous to the souls under his protection, but self-possessed and aloof as a ruler. He owned the Cwn Annwn—the Hounds of Annwn, a pack of hunting dogs with white bodies and red ears—and rode with them through the sky from fall to early spring. Exactly what he was hunting is a matter of debate. Some say he sought the souls of the dead who had lost their way to Annwn, or those who clung too fiercely to the mortal world. Others thought he might be rounding up the spirits of those who'd been tempted away from the Otherworld by curiosity about the lives of mortals. He hunted from Samhain to Beltain, the two times of the year when the boundaries between the Otherworld and the mortal world grew thin, so either reason may be true.

Arawn is protective of what he sees as his property, and willing to fight to retrieve what has been stolen. He regards reliability and nobility of action as paramount virtues. In the ancient tales, Pwyll, lord of Dyfed, hunted a stag that had rightly belonged to Arawn. To make amends, Pwyll took Arawn's place in combat. Later Pwyll did not give in to temptation but slept "chastely" with Arawn's wife. As a reward for such noble deeds, Arawn befriended Pwyll. Being able to claim the Lord of the Otherworld as a friend was of considerable benefit to Pwyll.

Arawn's province is nobility of word and deed, truthfulness, and protection and security. His symbol is a running dog.

Morrigan

The Morrigan is the Celtic goddess of war, death, sex, and fertility. Like the Great Mother, she's a triple goddess. But unlike her, Morrigan is a shape-shifter, changing her appearance to confuse and terrify soldiers on the battlefield. The three goddesses who make up the triple are Morrigan (Phantom Queen), Nemhain (Battle Frenzy), and Badhbh (Crow or Raven), the carrion bird that feasts on the bodies of the slain.

The Morrigan is both terrifyingly beautiful and profoundly frightening. Proud, powerful, and often violent, she is a source of fear and awe. Amoral and pitiless, Morrigan symbolizes directed aggression, the use of power to achieve a goal regardless of the consequences. Yet the death she brings clears away the old to make way for the new.

The Morrigan is the spirit of revolution, of the violent overthrowing of the old order and the ushering in of the hope of a brighter future. It is painful, but without her actions all things stagnate and decay. Her symbol is the dagger, crow, or raven. It is also the "tribal" tattoo.

Taranis

Taranis symbolizes authority. A powerful elemental deity, Taranis is the Celtic thunder god. The low rumble of thunder rolling around the hills is the sound of his chariot wheels racing across the sky. He controls weather and storms, and is especially associated with the forces of change. Pitiless and quick to anger, his word is law, and he will ruthlessly cut down all who oppose him.

At the same time, he often brings refreshment. The rain that comes with thunder satisfies the parched land. The violence of his storms, while deeply unpleasant at the time, clears the air of tension and releases stress. Nevertheless he should be approached with caution, and will expect recompense for any action he may take on his devotees' behalf. Taranis was associated with human sacrifice by burning—unsurprising, perhaps, since lightning accompanies a thunderstorm and so was one of his attributes.

Like Daghdha, Taranis would have been revered by the Druids. His attributes are command and belligerence, the ability to face up to and overcome hostility by the power of his personality. His symbol is a solar wheel with lightning coming from it.

Manannan

Manannan mac Lir (Manawydan son of Llyr in the Welsh tradition) was a sea deity, sometimes perceived as the god who ushered the souls of the dead to the Otherworld Isle of the Blessed (another name for Annwn). His ship, *Wave Sweeper*, needed no sails to skim the sea. Manannan owned a cloak that could envelop him in mists, allowing him—and perhaps those with him—to pass unseen. He was the original possessor of a goblet of truth that would break if lies were uttered before it and become magically restored if truth was spoken.

Traditionally, Manannan was considered a good and just deity, dealing fairly with the humans with whom he came into contact. His association with the Otherworld and its hidden knowledge, and his ownership of the goblet of truth, suggest, however, he was not easily deceived, and may punish those who dealt unfairly with others.

Manannan's skills are navigation by the stars, control of the weather at sea, and the ability to create shrouding fogs. His attributes are clear-sightedness, foresight, and serenity. His symbol is a wave, or a boat without sails.

Sulis

Sulis was the local goddess of the springs at what is now known as Bath, in south-west England. The geothermal springs here run at over 104°F (40°C) and are the hottest in the country. From earliest times, they have provided hot water from underground, which would have seemed a miracle to all who visited. The mineral-laden waters were believed to be a source of healing. The legend is that King Bladud (who gave his name to the town of Bath) bathed in the spring and was cured of leprosy. As a consequence, the springs became celebrated not only in the British Isles but throughout Europe. During their time of occupation in England, the Romans built a temple complex around the springs, much of which can still be seen and explored. The springs have remained famous throughout their history.

The Romans considered Sulis to be a local version of their own deity, Minerva. Sulis was a goddess of healing and prophecy—the fact that she presided over hot water bubbling up from underground meant she was intimately associated with the mysteries of the Otherworld, often reached by a portal into the earth. Small votive images of the afflicted parts of the devotees' bodies were placed in the water, no doubt accompanied by prayers for healing. Lead and pewter "curse tablets" have also been found in the springs. These were thin sheets of metal, inscribed and folded or rolled and then dropped into the waters containing appeals to the goddess for vengeance against those who had committed some crime against the writer, usually thefts from the bathhouse itself. This implies that Sulis also dealt in divine justice, perhaps perceived as "healing" external wrongs as well as the illnesses of the body. The ills wished on the culprits may seem a little harsh today, including as they did a variety of physical and mental ailments and even death. Then again, given how much effort was involved in acquiring clothing or coin in ancient times, perhaps it's no surprise that theft was viewed so severely by the victims.

Sulis' attributes are healing, hidden knowledge, and justice. By extension, she can also be seen as presiding over science, reason, and decision-making. She is calm, serene, and rational. Her symbol is the eye.

Govannon

Much like his Roman counterpart Hephaestus, Govannon, while vitally important to the Celts, did not play a conspicuous role in their legends. He is the smith god who created the mighty weapons that gave them mastery in battle. As such he was very much a warrior's deity. His Irish counterpart, Goibniu, was credited with inventing the art of brewing—his ale gave immortality.

Powerful and knowledgeable, Govannon's attributes are strength and skill, the ability to shape weaponry and useful objects from the raw metal of the earth. His symbol is a hammer.

Ogmios

Depicted as an old, bald man, Ogmios is the god of eloquence, incantation, and poetry. His powers are innate. He's sometimes portrayed with fine chains connecting his tongue to the ears of the humans around him, indicating the irresistible power of his verbal skills. He is the archetypal smooth-talker who can convince anyone of anything, but he isn't malicious. His words bring joy and gladness of spirit, and make possible reconciliation and declarations of love.

His Irish counterpart, Ogma, was credited with inventing Ogham, the writing system made up of straight line "runes" that comprise what is sometimes called the Celtic "alphabet." This was mostly used, however, for recording genealogies. While they were important to the individuals involved, they have been of little use to us.

Ogmios symbolizes communication and the ability to influence others. It is a skill that should be used with caution and not for ill-doing. His symbol is the Ogham rune for O (pictured right).

Cernunnos

Cernunnos is the Horned One, the supreme Lord of the Wildwood. He is portrayed as a man with the antlers of a stag. Also known as "Herne the Hunter," his is a free, unfettered elemental spirit, rejoicing in life and all it brings, good or bad. It's all part of the "Great Dance," the eternal cycle of existence, and is to be accepted as such. He is a god not only of hunting but also of fertility. Cernunnos is a fierce deity, unpredictable and untameable.

Cernunnos watches over all wild animals, but particularly those with horns and hooves. One of his principle tasks is to maintain the balance of life in nature. He decides which animals are strong and fit enough to survive and breed, and culls the rest, thus preventing overpopulation, stagnation, and weakness in the animal population.

Cernunnos's attributes are forceful action, an intimate understanding of the need for balance and stability in nature as well as within oneself, and the necessity for sacrifice for the good of all. His symbol is himself.

Epona

The horse goddess Epona was greatly revered by the Celts. Horses represented both wealth and status. They were the main means for travel and battle. Celtic warriors were renowned horsemen, and devoted to Epona as a particularly warrior-orientated aspect of the Great Goddess. Statues of Epona frequently show her riding side-saddle, accompanied by foals as a symbol of the fertility and prosperity she bestowed.

Epona symbolizes nature gently controlled and working in harmony with the human race. Her symbol is the horse.

Dylan Eil Don

Dylan was the first of Arianrhod's twins to be born, and was a big, golden-haired child. As soon as Math ap Mathonwy, a king of Gwynedd, named him, he headed for the sea, diving in and receiving its spirit. Afterward he spent his whole time there, able to swim as fast as the fastest fish. Little is known about him, although he may be associated with the seal—the seal, too, is a very fast swimmer, as seen in the legend of the *selkie*. This half-human/half-seal creature assumed a man's shape simply by removing his seal skin. The transformation of human into animal plays a significant part in Celtic legend. However, since so little is known about Dylan, it's impossible to be sure. We do know that he was accidentally killed by his uncle Govannon with a single blow. This could be taken to mean that Dylan wasn't in human shape at the time. Alternatively, it could simply mean he was mistaken for someone else or was not clearly seen in the water. His death was widely mourned, however, and Govannon grieved deeply, so it's safe to assume Dylan was a well-known and well-loved character.

Dylan embodies the mystery and allure of the sea, its unpredictable and profound nature. His accidental death at the hand of the smith god may be seen as the fragility of the natural world when faced with the tools of man's dominion, and act as a warning to those who think they can destroy with impunity. His symbol is a seal.

Rosmerta

Also known as the Good Provider, Rosmerta is the goddess of overflowing abundance and the fertility of the earth. Fruit and vegetation are in her particular care, along with the associated foods of honey and herbs.

Rosmerta's attributes are hospitality, generosity, prosperity, and open-handedness. She is tolerant, kindly, and warmly welcoming. Her symbol is the cornucopia.

LLeu Llaw Gyffes

Lleu Llaw Gyffes—"fair one of the skilled hand"—was the second-born of Arianrhod's twins. At his birth he was a formless blob that Gwydion swept up and kept in a chest—a sort of substitute womb—until he developed into a child. Furious, Arianrhod refused to acknowledge the boy, placing three *tynghedau* (curses) upon him, namely that he should have no name except the one she

gave him, he could carry no weapons unless she armed him herself, and he could never marry a human woman. These essentially denied him his humanity, taking away his status, recognition and all possibility of advance or family. Gwydion managed to trick his sister into breaking the first two *tynghedau*, and with Math created Blodeuwedd out of flowers to be Lleu's wife.

Blodeuwedd fell in love with Gronw Pebr, a hunter and lord of a neighboring land, and together they plotted to kill Lleu. Being the son of a goddess, however, Lleu was very difficult to harm. He could not be killed during the day or night, neither indoors nor outdoors, not riding, nor on foot, and not by any weapon lawfully made. Blodeuwedd tricked the method by which he could be killed out of her husband, but Lleu changed into an eagle to escape death. Gwydion later returned him to human form and transformed Blodeuwedd into an owl as punishment for her treachery.

Lleu Llaw Gyffes symbolizes the outcast, the exile, the refugee, the nameless, and the socially excluded. He finally assumed his rightful place, but required powerful help to do so. His symbol is the eagle.

Gwydion

The Welsh magician and trickster Gwydion was one of Arianrhod's two brothers. A powerful god, Gwydion was hardly the most admirable of deities. Math ap Mathonwy, a king of Gwynedd, was forced to sit with his feet in the

lap of a virgin, Goewin, when not at war, or he would die. Gwydion's brother, Gilfaethwy, took a fancy to Goewin. Together, the two brothers plotted to ensure Math was away, waging war with Pryderi, Lord of Dyfedd, so that Gilfaethwy could rape Goewin. Math discovered what had happened as soon as he arrived back and tried to rest his feet in Goewin's lap. As a punishment, he banished the brothers for three years, cursing them to turn into deer, wolves, and finally pigs, swapping genders as they swapped forms. They produced three offspring who were later transformed into humans.

Gwydion symbolizes duplicity and the intimate understanding of opposites. His lessons are difficult but result in a greater comprehension of the world and one's place within it. His symbol is the Celtic knot.

The Druids

The Druids were the judges, scientists, priests, astronomers, and poets of their time. Wise and immensely powerful men and women, they had freedom to travel throughout Celtic lands in return for their services as lawgivers, seers, and priests.

Druids taught the doctrine of the immortality of the soul. Their training was exclusive and very demanding, taking many years. It included lessons in two other disciplines of the intellectual elite: Druids were also Bards, who sang the history and legends of the people, and Vates, soothsayers, fortune-tellers, and

what would today be called psychotherapists. Druids were perfectly able to read and write, but were forbidden to record their knowledge, being required to memorize all that was passed down to them. This may have been a ploy to prevent others from accessing this wisdom (and thereby diminishing the Druids' authority) but was equally likely to be a form of mental discipline, designed to focus the mind and develop the memory.

Druids were exempt from taxation and armed service. They held authority over kings, and weren't afraid to wield their power. Rulers were often chosen by the Druids for their skill, strength, and personal abilities instead of the title passing from father to son. Appeals to their wisdom often settled inter-tribal conflicts and so would have saved lives otherwise lost in battle. On the other hand, they also routinely pronounced judgment on criminals, who could be condemned to agonising deaths by being burned alive, or by drowning or disembowelment.

The Druid symbolizes the conscious shifting of knowledge into action, the use of what has been learned to effect change in the outside world. Symbols of the Druids are the double spiral or the world tree, its roots deep underground in the Otherworld, its sturdy trunk supporting life, and its branches brushing the sky.

Rhiannon

Rhiannon first appeared as a beautiful woman richly attired in golden brocade and riding a pure white horse. Intensely curious, Pwyll, Lord of Dyfed, sent his best horseman after her. The speed of the chase exhausted the pursuer's horse—yet her great horse strolled serenely on. Rhiannon allowed Pwyll himself to draw level with her, however, and she told him that she wanted to marry him, and not the man to whom she had been forcibly betrothed. Between them, Pwyll and Rhiannon tricked her betrothed into setting her free a year later. Rhiannon has been associated with horses and with the moon—her horse symbolizes the moon, for although it seems to move slowly across the sky, no man can ever draw alongside it (on earth, anyway). The mirror also represents the symbol of the moon.

Rhiannon represents beauty, fidelity, and love. Her symbol is a round mirror, representing her great beauty and the moon.

Blodeuwedd

Originally Blodeuedd (the name meaning "flowers"), Blodeuwedd was created from the flowers of broom, meadowsweet, and oak by Math and his magician nephew Gwydion to be the wife of Lleu Llaw Gyffes. Understandably, Blodeuedd didn't take kindly to this betrothal and had an adulterous affair with Gronw Pebr. Blodeuedd tricked the secret of how to kill her husband from Lleu himself, not an easy task, since he was the son of the goddess Arianrhod. Gronw struck Lleu in the side with a spear, but Lleu escaped when Gwydion turned him into an eagle. As punishment for Blodeuedd's treachery, Gwydion changed her into an owl, "the bird all other birds hate" and her name to Blodeuwedd, which means "flower face." This refers to the owl's appearance—the face of a tawny owl in particular looks as though it's surrounded by petals. Gronw is punished by receiving the same fate that he had intended for Lleu. Not being a god, he is killed.

Blodeuwedd is a powerful figure, perhaps more so as the owl, the queen of the night, than as the flower maiden. She symbolizes self-determination, female power, intrigue, and secrets. She will not be dictated to, and will go her own way despite the risks involved—and by doing so she effects her own transformation. Her symbol is an owl face, which resembles a flower.

Taliesin

The tale of how Taliesin came to be is bound closely with the tale of his mother Ceridwen, the keeper of the Cauldron of the Otherworld, in which divine inspiration and knowledge were brewed. Ceridwen had a son, the grotesquely ugly Avagddu, and she planned to give him a potion that would imbue him with wisdom, eloquence, and inner charm in order to offset his appearance. To that end she had her young servant, Gwion, stir the potion, making sure the ingredients were properly mixed. Gwion, however, managed to spill three drops of it onto his hand. Automatically bringing the scalded skin to his mouth, he ingested the three drops and instantly gained the wisdom and knowledge that had been intended for Avagddu.

Aware that Ceridwen would be furious, Gwion ran for his life. Ceridwen followed, hunting him remorselessly. In his fear he became a hare to put her off the scent. She became a hound and chased him. He leapt into the river, becoming a fish, but she transformed herself into an otter. Desperate to escape, he changed into a bird, but she became a hawk and flew after him. Finally, he turned himself into an ear of corn, whereupon Ceridwen became a hen and swallowed the seed, which impregnated her. Her child was Taliesin. Ceridwen would have killed him at birth but he was so beautiful she was unable to do so and cast him into the sea in a leather bag to live or die at fate's bidding.

Taliesin is, therefore, twice born (once as Gwion and a second time as Taliesin) and, effectively, his own father! He has experienced the three realms of earth—water, air, and earth itself—and imbibed divine wisdom. It's not really any wonder that he became the best and most skilled of bards.

Taliesin is a handsome man, seemingly forever young, affectionate, chivalrous, and tolerant. He symbolizes all the best qualities of the human race, its creativity, imagination, and ability to communicate. His symbol is the salmon of wisdom.

Boudica

Boudica was the widowed queen of the Iceni tribe. She lived during the latter period of the Roman occupation of Britain. The Roman historian Cassius Dio describes her as being very tall with tawny hair that reached her hips, fierce eyes, and a loud, harsh voice. She habitually wore a multi-colored tunic and a thick cloak fastened with a brooch, a golden torc around her neck to indicate her status, and her weapon of choice was a spear. She was exceptionally intelligent, but since she was probably a Druidess as well as a queen—or at least had received Druidic training—this is perhaps not so surprising. She objected to the Romans' wholesale looting of her people's land and belongings, which was viewed as insurrection by the occupiers. As punishment she was stripped and whipped like a common criminal—and her two virgin daughters were enslaved and raped.

Such a horrific insult could not go unavenged, and the kingdom exploded in revolt. The occupying Romans found themselves under sustained and vicious attack. Tens of thousands of the Roman forces were killed, and many ordinary citizens—Romans who had settled in Britain—taken captive. If the historians are to be believed, many of these were tortured. Boudica herself had a hand in this, sacrificing female captives to the war goddess Andraste in sacred groves by impaling them, naked, lengthwise, and leaving them to die—a grisly fate, but perhaps understandable retribution for the treatment handed out to Britons under Roman rule. At the end, the warrior queen took poison and died rather than face capture by her enemy.

Boudica, whose name means Victorious, symbolizes the freedom fighter, the rebel, the warrior who fights with whatever weapon comes to hand in the cause of liberty and freedom from oppression. Her symbol is the triqueta enclosed within a circle.

Cúchulain

Cúchulain, the legendary Irish Celtic warrior, was the nephew of the Irish king Conor, son of Dechtire and the god Lugh, who visited Dechtire on her wedding night in the form of a fly, and wooed her and her fifty attendant maidens away.

Cúchulain's original name was Setanta. He acquired the name Cúchulain "Hound of Culain"—when he killed a great dog belonging to Culain the smith, in self-defense. To make amends, he volunteered to act as a watchdog in the hound's place while a replacement was trained.

Cúchulain was a good-looking youth who grew into a handsome man, so much so that other warriors were worried about the influence he would have over their wives and daughters. Cúchulain was strong and powerful, and skilled in the arts of war, which were taught to him by the warrior woman Scáthach at her home, Dún Scáith, on the island of Skye. It was here that he was given a fearsome barbed spear called Gáe Bulg. The spear was made from the bone of a sea monster and was invariably lethal. He performed many feats of strength and skill throughout his short but adventurous life, and became known as the Champion of Ireland at an early age.

He is perhaps best known for his "warp-spasm," a frenzy that physically warped his body so that his muscles and sinews stood out in knots. He also became horrifyingly ugly—one eye appeared to bulge outward while the other seemed to recede into his head, his grimace reached back to his ears and his lips pulled back right over his teeth. In this state he was berserk, possessed of superhuman strength and ferocity, unable to tell friend from foe, becoming a terrifying figure simply intent on battle and indiscriminate killing.

Cúchulain symbolizes strength, endurance, and single-minded dedication. His symbol is the spear.

Carry Your Guide Symbols

One way to emulate the Celts is to wear Guide symbols as talismans. These silver or gold images remind the wearer of the attributes and essence of its possessor. As earrings, pendants on neckchains, brooches, or bracelets, the symbol can invoke the chosen Guide, allowing the wearer to draw on the skills and talents needed.

Perhaps you are preparing for a test or examination of some kind. Which would be the most useful skill—Sulis's calm rationality and pure knowledge, or the Druid's wisdom and ability to apply it? Or perhaps you need to confront someone to resolve an unpleasant situation. Would Daghdha's sense of humor be useful to defuse the tension, or do you need Arianrhod's help to understand the other person's motivation and purpose? Perhaps both? There's no need to restrict yourself to one Guide.

Talismans can be seen as good-luck charms. Of course, the power to invoke luck, success, or anything else does not reside in an image, but they can be very useful for focusing the mind on attaining the desired result.

Chapter 3
Ogham: Celtic Alphabet

The Druids may not have committed any of their vast store of knowledge and wisdom to the written word, but the Celts in general were certainly not illiterate. Along with their own languages, Greek was used for trade, and even before the Roman occupation, Mediterranean culture and the Latin language were encroaching into the Celtic population in Southern Europe. However, the closest we have to an original Celtic alphabet is Ogham.

Ogham Inscriptions

The characters were inscribed along either side of a continuous line. It's not a particularly elegant or user-friendly alphabet. It looks more like a code, and it has been suggested that was exactly how Ogham was used, in some circumstances. The Ogham characters would be easy to scratch into wood, or mark out with the fingers against another object or even the hand, rather like sign-language today. Originally, Ogham would probably have been written and read from the bottom up, the way you would climb a tree, and from left to right, following the direction of the sun and moon across the heavens in the northern hemisphere. Some inscriptions are etched into the edge of stones, keeping to the curve of the monument.

OGHAM ALPHABET

The inscriptions that have been found have mainly been carved on large stones—mostly names, marking genealogies, or sometimes the boundary between two tribal lands, only relevant to those involved. The vast majority of the population wouldn't even have been able to read. Reading and writing were skills reserved for the Druids, Bards, Vates, and some of the warrior nobles. After all, the only "reading" necessary for an agricultural community was natural—reading the weather and the seasons. Otherwise their skills were simply those required for growing crops and caring for livestock.

In legend, Ogma, the Irish god of eloquence, is credited with devising Ogham, probably to provide a way for those who hear him to record the beauty and splendor of his speech.

OGHAM U

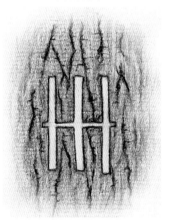

OGHAM SOURCES

It is unclear where Ogham came from, although it's plausible that it was created by the Druids. It was used mainly in Ireland and to a lesser extent in parts of Britain. We know all of it from three principal sources:

- As a section of the Irish "Book of Ballymote" (written around 1390) called the *Auraicept na n-Éces*, or scholar's primer, claimed to have been written in the seventh century by Irish monks.

- *In Lebor Ogaim*, the Ogham Tract, written sometime between the sixth and tenth centuries.

- *Bríatharogam*, again from sometime between the sixth and tenth centuries, is a list of "kennings"—figures of speech—of the Ogham characters.

Tree Alphabet

Ogham was popularized by Robert Graves in his work *The White Goddess*, in which he uses the "tree alphabet" devised by the late seventeenth-century Irish historian and antiquarian, Roderick O'Flaherty, in his history of Ireland. Using the various different "kennings" in the *Auraicept na n-Éces*, O'Flaherty allocated tree names to each of the letters. While some of the letters do correspond to tree names, not all of them do.

COMPARISON OF BRÍATHAROGAM
AND ROBERT GRAVES' ARBOREAL
ALPHABET (RIGHT)

		BRIATHAROGAM		ROBERT GRAVES	
		LETTER	TRANSLATION	LETTER	TRANSLATION
	B	beithe	birch	beithe	birch
	L	luis	blaze/herb	luis	rowan
	F	fern	alder	fer	fern
	S	sail	willow	sail	willow
	N	nion	fork/loft	nin	ash
	H	uath	fear (?)	huath	whitethorn
	D	dair	oak	duir	oak
	T	tinne	metal/rod	tinne	holly/elder
	C	coll	hazel	coll	hazel
	Q	ceirt	bush	ceirt	apple tree
	M	muin	neck	muinn	vine
	G	gort	field	gort	ivy
	NG	ngéatal	wounding (?)	getal	broom
	Z	straif	sulfur	straif	blackthorn
	R	ruis	redness	ruis	elder tree
	A	ailm	(uncertain)	ailm	pine tree
	O	onn	ash tree	onn	furze
	U	ur	earth	ur	heath
	E	eadhadh	(uncertain)	cdad	aspen
	I	iodhadh	(uncertain) i	dad	yew

The Forfeda

The original Ogham script consisted of just 20 characters. The characters known collectively as the *forfeda* were a much later addition and don't appear in any genuinely ancient inscriptions. They were created to allow for foreign words, but even so Ogham doesn't provide every letter of the modern English alphabet.

The final three forfeda characters—eite, spás, and eite thuathall—appear to act as a form of punctuation, the chevrons marking the beginning and end of a sentence while spás is a space between words.

Using Ogham

Ogham was probably devised and certainly extensively used in Ireland, so any inscriptions made using the alphabet should be in Primitive Irish. This, it seems, is about as close as we can come to the original Celtic language. Since that is clearly beyond the scope of this book, plain English will suffice. For this exercise—for ease of use and given the simplicity of the characters—it doesn't matter which way up the characters are, vertical or horizontal. The traditionally minded may prefer to write in columns from bottom to top. But if this is too difficult, write from left to right and in rows, as in modern English. An inscription in a spiral is also a possibility, circling inward to symbolize inner strength and tranquility, or outward for growth and development.

THE FORFEDA CHARACTERS

	LETTER		TRANSLATION
	EA	éabhadh	(uncertain)
	OI	or	gold
	UI	uilleann	elbow
	IA	ifin	pine
	AE	eamhancholl	double e
	P	peith	soft birch
		eite	feather
		spás	space
		eite thuathall	reversed feather

It's possible to substitute Ogham characters for most of the missing English letters phonetically. The Celtic "C" is usually a hard "K" sound, while the English soft "C" can be replaced with the Ogham for "S." For English "V," use Ogham "F," for "J" use "I" (as the Romans did), and for "Y" use "AE." "W" can be replaced by "UU" (literally double U), while the "X" sound can be made by using Ogham "C" and "S" together. It may take a little getting used to, but will become easier with practice. Alternatively, you might like to find the Irish or Welsh versions of the words you wish to spell, and try translating them into Ogham instead.

Make an Ogham Talisman

Decide, firstly, what purpose your inscription is going to serve. Your own name? An appeal to your favorite Guide? A particular wish or need? It's worth putting some time and effort into choosing, since the exercise will take a little effort and energy.

Are you going to carry the inscription with you? If so, would you rather carve it on to a piece of wood, write it on a piece of paper, or even have it inscribed on a piece of jewelry? How durable do you need the item to be? Wood is an excellent medium. It recalls the Táball-Lorg, the Poet's Staff, thought to be a series of flat wooden staves fastened together at the base. The staves opened out into a fan shape and would have been engraved with aide-memoires—Ogham mnemonics—to help the bard remember the works he was to perform. They would not have featured the poems and songs themselves. In addition, of course, wood comes from trees, which were sacred to the Druids and revered by the Celts as a whole.

Ideally, you should create your own talisman, from start to finish. Choose your inscription, the Guide you wish it to represent, if you so choose, the material you intend to use, and the shape you prefer—round for the solar deities, round or triangular for representations of the Great Goddess, square for the Daghdha. When choosing wood, try to use trees that were native to Britain in Celtic times, bearing in mind their innate qualities and symbolism (see page 92).

You might find it helpful to choose a wood that represents a character trait you feel you are lacking, to act as a talisman to help you bring forth that aspect of yourself, or perhaps to symbolize what you would like to happen in your future.

It's important not to hurry, but to relax and enjoy the work. In a small way, you'll be tapping into a uniquely Celtic experience—allow fellow-feeling to flow through you!

Chapter 4

Symbols from Domestic Life

Our basic needs haven't changed much over the ages, only the way we fulfill those requirements. We all still need shelter from the elements, a covering for warmth, food to keep the body alive, and a way to pass on our genes, much as any animal. As humans, however, we also need companionship, fellow-feeling, emotional fulfillment, security, and a strong foundation for our children and loved ones—and a sense of purpose, a way of satisfying our drive to explore, goals to reach, and fellow minds with whom to share our thoughts and ideas, hopes, and dreams.

We have lost much of the warmth and companionship, security and sense of belonging that was such a feature of Celtic life, simply because of the way we live today. Often separated from family by distance or by our work, many of us may feel as though there's something essential missing from our lives. Drawing inspiration from the ordinary Celts' way of life may help to ease that sense of something lacking by drawing us back to a deeper appreciation of the earth that nourishes our body and the love and friendship that nurtures our spirit.

Hearth-fire

The hearth-fire was literally at the heart of the Celtic home. It was built in the center of the roundhouse, its heat and light spreading out equally to be shared by everyone within, and it was never allowed to go out—to allow such a thing was a terrible disgrace.

The hearth-fire was also where the food was cooked that nourished the family, stewed in the cauldron, heated on the stones that formed its base and contained it, or baked in the embers. It also provided the heat for the bread oven, in the larger roundhouses.

The hearth-fire symbolizes the heart, the source of emotional warmth, nurture, and compassion. It represents the Mother, her love and protection, the security the child feels held in her arms.

Cauldron

To the Celts, the cauldron was a symbol of the Great Mother's womb, providing all good things and causing regeneration and rebirth, as the burgeoning life of the spring followed the cold bleakness of the winter. It could be as simple as a cooking pot over the household fire, or as elaborate as the ceremonial silver cauldron discovered at Gundestrup, Denmark in 1891.

There are a number of cauldrons in Celtic myth and legend. The Daghdha's cauldron never ran dry, and all who ate from it went away wholly satisfied. The cauldron of Bran the Blessed not only fed all who came to it, it could also bring the dead back to life—which made it a fearsome weapon in the hands of an army, as all the slain warriors could be rejuvenated, although unfortunately they didn't regain the power of speech. While this would have made them a terrifying and eerie enemy, it also suggests that something is lost in such unnatural regeneration, a certain power of communication, the loss of the ability to share knowledge.

Ceridwen's cauldron, which brewed a potion that would give the drinker all the wit and wisdom in the world (see Taliesin, page 53), symbolized divine inspiration and knowledge rather than physical nourishment. Taliesin's poem "Spoils of Annwn" speaks of the Cauldron of Annwn, the property of the chief of the Otherworld. It was richly decorated and rimmed with pearls, kept warm by the breath of nine maidens, and would not cook a coward's food—although whether this means it would refuse to cook the food of a coward or whether it removed the trait of cowardice from an individual isn't clear.

The cauldron was a central, ever-present part of Celtic life. Into it went meat, vegetables, grain, herbs, and berries, and out of it was ladled life-preserving

stews and broths. It would have been kept simmering nearly all of the time, as the first thing a Celt did on receiving visitors was to offer them food. Such hospitality was of vital importance, reaffirming the close-knit nature of normal Celtic society.

The cauldron symbolizes all that was most generous in Celtic life — hospitality, the nourishment of body, mind, and spirit. It also symbolizes renewal, rebirth, and the creation of life.

Honey

While a wide variety of spices and condiments were known in the ancient world, the average Celt in a northern community would have little access to the more exotic and expensive flavorings that trade with Greece and Rome could provide. Native herbs and vegetation were used to make food more palatable, and to add sweetness to foods there were birch sap and honey.

The collecting of honey can be a risky operation. Honeybees will attack anything that threatens the hive, and their barbed stingers inject a surprisingly powerful apitoxin, which affects the nerves. One sting is unlikely to do more than be painful, unless the victim is one of the small number of the population now allergic to bee stings, but many stings is a different matter, and can be fatal. The person who brought the wild honeycomb safely back to the community would be considered as much a hunter—in a small way—as the one who brought back the boar.

Honey has been used medicinally for thousands of years. Employed topically, it is disinfectant and antibacterial, and promotes the growth of new skin, making it a good, if messy, treatment for wounds. Drunk in hot water it soothes sore throats, and may help alleviate the symptoms of bronchial ailments. As the physicians of their day, the Druids would have been skilled in its various uses.

It's likely that the Celts started using beehives made of wicker and daub to keep bees from quite early in their history—bee-keeping dates possibly from as long ago as 6,000 BCE.

Its most extravagant use was in the making of mead. Pure mead was brewed from honey, naturally occurring yeast and water, but the taste could vary quite dramatically depending on which flowers provided the nectar for the bees.

Other ingredients could be added to vary the taste—berries such as wild strawberries, blackberries, or crushed rosehips; flower petals such as wild rose; meadowsweet, which would add a hint of vanilla; or fruit such as crab apples (apple mead was known as cyser in later centuries). For Celtic nobles on the south coast of England and on the Continent, expensive traded spices, such as ginger, cinnamon, and nutmeg, could be added, and fruits such as grapes.

Given the length of time it took to ferment—a minimum of six months, and strong, sweet sack mead could take years—and the difficulty of gathering the main ingredient, mead was generally the drink of warriors and kings. But it was also a drink for lovers. The term honeymoon traditionally comes from the belief that a man and woman eating honey or drinking mead for a full month before marriage would become more fertile—and nine months after their union a strong and healthy child would result.

Honey symbolizes all the sweetnesses in life, its joys and achievements.

Bread

Oats were used to make oatcakes, wheat to make flat breads, and risen loaves would have been baked in a small clay oven or kiln to one side of the central fire. The Celts may well have learned the skill of using brewing yeast from beer in their bread dough from their neighbors the Gauls; it was reputed to give a lighter texture to the end product. Different quantities of different flours would be added to produce different tastes. Bread was the primary source of carbohydrates in the Celtic diet, and would most likely have accompanied every meal.

MAKE YOUR OWN

It's impractical to suggest making a meal entirely from scratch, even if we have the necessary hunting and farming skills, but a lesser task is well within the capabilities of most people. Try making a loaf of bread.

Use stone-ground spelt flour if possible. It's closer to the Celtic original, and has a nuttier flavor than whole-wheat. It rises a little more quickly too, and doesn't need to rise twice to make an excellent bread. In Celtic times the grains were milled with a quern—one stone grinding against another—but again, that's a little impractical in the modern home. If spelt flour isn't available, use stone-ground whole-wheat instead.

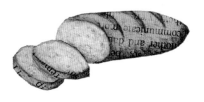

There are as many different variations of bread recipes as there are bakers, but this is a simple, basic method. You could try adding extra ingredients to vary the flavor—poppy seeds, sesame seeds, sunflower, and/or pumpkin seeds. A little grated onion or grated Cheddar cheese are also excellent additions. These quantities make a small "first-timer" loaf. For larger loaves, double the quantities.

1 ½ cups (360 g) all-purpose flour—spelt or whole-wheat
Good pinch of salt
4 fl oz (120 ml) warm water
Small flat teaspoon of active dry bread yeast,
or 1 oz (30 g) of fresh yeast
Large teaspoon of honey

Dissolve the honey in the warm water and add the yeast, leaving it somewhere warm—a sunny windowsill, or near a radiator—to activate. When the water has turned a dull muddy gray-fawn color and the top is covered with a thick scum, it's ready.

Put the flour and salt in a large mixing bowl and add the yeast and water. Stir for a moment to mix, then knead with your hands, using a folding and pressing motion. It's almost impossible to over-knead whole-wheat flour, but spelt flour must be kneaded quickly and lightly or the bread will be heavy and crumbly—a maximum of four minutes is enough. For a whole-wheat loaf, cover the dough with a warm damp cloth and leave somewhere warm to rise until it has doubled in size. Punch down to deflate the dough and knead again. Then place the dough in a standard loaf tin or, for a more authentic loaf, shape it roughly into a domed circle or oval, place on a baking sheet, cover lightly, and

leave to double in size. For a spelt loaf, cover the bowl with a warm damp cloth for 15 minutes, then shape gently without further kneading, place the dough in the tin or on the sheet and bake.

Preheat the oven to 325°F/165°C/Gas 3 and place the bread on the middle shelf. Bake for 45 minutes to an hour, or until the top is browned. To check, gently knock the bottom of the loaf with your knuckles: it will sound faintly hollow, a little like a drum, when cooked.

For an extra-crusty spelt loaf, turn off the oven and leave the loaf for five minutes. Remove from the oven, place on a cooling rack, and try not to eat immediately, or all at once.

Bread symbolizes the basic stuff of life, those fundamental things needed to sustain us on our journey through our own lives—the plain requirements such as simple wholesome food, enough sleep, and the companionship of our peers.

The Loom

Weaving is a very ancient craft, known for millennia. It freed humans from the need to prepare animal skins for clothing, among other things. Flax for linen is probably the oldest known material used in the manufacture of cloth, possibly dating back ten thousand years. Wool began to be used a little later, both in its felted form and woven. The Celts used both, but it's likely that the farther north they lived, the more their clothing was based on wool, simply because of its greater warmth.

Women were usually responsible for weaving all the cloth, which was mainly used for clothing. Bedding was generally made of sheepskin for warmth and comfort, although it's possible that higher-status Celts might have had woven blankets. Every home had its own loom, a simple upright wooden frame with the warp threads held straight by weights, usually shaped stones with a hole through the middle. Given its importance in the family, the loom would most likely have been highly decorated and well looked after.

Historical records suggest that the Celts used bright colors made from vegetable dyes, and wove boldly checked and striped cloth. Needles of iron or bone were used to sew the clothing, with the seam on the inside, and the borders often decorated with additional colored thread, beads or small metal discs if the individual was wealthy or high-status.

Women usually wore an ankle-length dress, pinned at both shoulders with brooches if it had no sleeves. Men wore pants to the ankle, with a thigh or knee length tunic. Both often wore a woven or leather belt around the waist, from which a pouch could be suspended. Outside, a cloak would be worn, pinned at one shoulder with a brooch—a simple linen fabric for summer, with a much heavier cloak providing warmth in the winter. Celtic cloaks were famed, it appears, for their sturdy construction and weatherproof qualities. The inner layer was warm, the brightly patterned outer layer oiled with lanolin, the naturally waterproof grease obtained from sheep fleece.

The loom symbolizes control over the fabric of your life, the ability to change any element of it you desire, to bring color and pattern into your environment or your personality. It represents independence of ideas and the capability to go your own way, be individual and vibrant with your own style instead of following the herd.

Torc

The torc was a uniquely Celtic piece of jewelry, worn only by those of high status, the value of the metal used reflecting the status of the person wearing it—gold for kings, chiefs or, probably, Druids, silver for champions, bronze or iron for warriors. Celtic deities were usually shown wearing a torc, to symbolize their importance. The more elaborate might be awarded to a champion for heroism in battle, the simpler worn as a badge of status. Torcs were worn by both men and women.

The torc symbolizes the responsibilities and demands placed on the civilized human being—especially when in a position of leadership.

Brooch

Until the invention of buttons, most clothing was held closed either by belts or by brooches. Brooches have been employed for thousands of years, the first designs being simple, but the craft of their manufacture, and the skill with which they were decorated, grew over the millennia. By the time Celtic culture was flourishing they had become beautiful works of art in gold, silver, or bronze, masterfully shaped, delicately patterned and worn ostentatiously to display the owner's wealth, style, and artistic appreciation.

To wear the brooch, the spike-ended bar, which is attached to the main part of the brooch by a loop, was moved until the spike fitted through the opening, pushed through the layers of fabric to be pinned, then brought back through the opening and slid to one side, holding the fabric firm and displaying the brooch to best advantage. Women's dresses were held closed at each shoulder by a pair of brooches, while men's and women's cloaks were closed at one shoulder by the individual's most richly decorated brooch.

The brooch symbolizes joining together, uniting, making connections. It's a strong and vibrant symbol for anyone, but particularly for those involved in negotiations, counseling, or any of the mental health services where a deeper understanding of the mind is needed.

Rings and Other Adornments

Rings were popular items of jewelry, mostly worn by women—and it seems that toe-rings were the norm, rather than finger rings. They would have been made of silver, gold, bronze, or iron with incised patterns and possibly enameled decoration, and they would have been treasured possessions, quite possibly passed down from mothers to daughters.

Personal ornaments weren't only made of metal—bracelets could have been carved from wood, and nuts and dried seeds threaded together made attractive necklaces for those unable to afford more expensive jewelry. Stone was also used—shale from the south coast of England was worked into armlets and bracelets using a lathe, and traded both within the British Isles and on the Continent. Malachite, and the amber that occasionally washed up on the shore, made beautiful beads, and the Celts were also adept at making small glass beads, often with a simple pattern, which could be strung for bracelets or necklets, or braided into the hair. There were nephrite jade deposits in what became Switzerland and the Netherlands, and the lovely green stone may have been worked into jewelry. Its color alone would have linked it with the natural world and the Great Mother.

Jewelry symbolizes personal choice, and the freedom to make our own decisions. Often a sign of our entry into a different phase or stage of our lives, our choice of jewelry often shows our affinity to a particular peer group, person, religion, or spiritual path. It often changes over time, as we change allegiances or beliefs, but it is always a deeply personal symbol of ourselves.

Dagger and Sword

The Celts were superior swordsmen, their method of hacking and chopping at their enemies terrifying to their opponents. They used two types of sword, both made of iron—a long, slashing weapon, the largest of which would require two hands to use, and a shorter stabbing sword for hand-to-hand combat. A unique feature was the "human shaped" hilt, with "arms" and "legs" and a head for the pommel.

The sword was used by kings, chiefs, warriors, and Druids. The rest of the adult population carried a small dagger. Very much a utility object, it was used for cutting up food, or spearing it to eat, slicing nuts and berries from bushes, for general purposes, and for any task that needed a blade, or if necessary for defense.

The sword is an aggressive symbol, representing the willingness to attack. It should be used reluctantly and with great care. The dagger, on the other hand, symbolizes self-defense, and the fortitude to stand up for yourself. We do not, as a rule and quite rightly, carry weapons with us these days, but as a talisman a dagger or sword image, in the form of a piece of jewelry perhaps, can act to strengthen our courage and determination.

Gaming Board

That the Celts played board games is no great surprise: Every civilization has developed its own such games, from the Senet of ancient Egypt, the Sumerian Royal Game of Ur, the Icelandic Hnefatafl, Persian Shaturanga (arguably the ancestor of chess), to Japanese Go, which is reputed to have been devised over two thousand years BCE.

Archaeological excavations at Stanway in the UK have uncovered the graves of a warrior and a Druid doctor—their occupations deduced from the other goods in their graves—which both contained the remains of a gaming board.

Although we have no definite instructions for how the game was played, there are hints—asides, almost—in historical writings. The Roman writer Piso described a game that might have been played on a board like this: it involved "capturing" the opponent's pieces between two of one's own, a little like a simplified version of Go. The winner was the first to ensnare all of the other's pieces.

As with many such games, it taught the player to think in tactical, and maybe also strategic, terms. It may have been played by warriors as a teaching tool—as well as a non-violent way to fight—and by others as a means of relaxation.

The gaming board symbolizes the ability to think coolly and critically to overcome the problems at hand. It represents forward planning, considering the consequences of our actions and adjusting our methods —or our goals—accordingly.

Harp

The harp is a very ancient instrument, dating from at least 4,000 BCE in Egypt, and quite possibly a lot earlier. While its origins are unknown, it has been conjectured that the instrument was inspired by the sound of a bow-string reverberating after an arrow had been fired. The earliest instruments comprised an L-shaped frame with the strings strung diagonally between the struts. The third solid side was added much later. The strings were made of animal gut, and the range would have been fairly limited. Later Celtic harps had between 19 and 40 strings, averaging around 34. It's likely that the earliest Celtic harps had fewer strings. The original design of harp was small enough to be carried easily, and played by resting it between the knees and against the right shoulder. It's played with the thumb and first three fingers of each hand—the little finger is too short and usually too weak to be used effectively.

The harp would not have been a common household item except in the home of a Bard. Song and music were essentials at any feast or festival and Bards were the celebrities of their time, honored and revered throughout society, singing the tales of the gods and the exploits of the heroes of the past.

The harp symbolizes artistry and skill in creative matters, the crafting of disparate elements into a beautiful and harmonious whole. It embodies the ability to inspire others, to appeal to all that's best within the human soul, and bring that goodness to the surface where it can find expression.

Chariot and Wagon

The chariots we know of from archaeological finds and historical writings were used for combat. Light, wooden, two-wheeled vehicles pulled by two horses, they were very fast and maneuverable in battle. They held two people, the warrior him or herself and a driver, who needed to be skilled in handling the horses and the chariot, and was usually drawn from the general populace.

The chariot was harnessed to the horses by a single pole and a yoke. We have legends of warriors running along the pole, standing on the yoke over the horses' necks, and attacking the opposing warriors from that elevated position—which would require both considerable skill and an excellent sense of balance, and have been terrifying to the enemy. Most often, however, as described by Caesar in his *Gallic War*, the chariot was used to get warriors into the thick of the battle, then raced out of the way ready to be used in the event of retreat.

The wagon was a very different vehicle. Sturdy, made of wood and not overly fast, it was designed to move heavy loads and would have been pulled by a team of oxen. Like the chariot, it used a single pole and yoke to control the team, but it had four wheels instead of two. Given the work and expense

involved in making a wagon, it may be that these vehicles were owned communally and used for moving large and heavy items between villages or for trading purposes.

Both chariot and wagon symbolize purposeful movement, but while the chariot represents speedy travel in short bursts, the wagon is a symbol of more businesslike, long-term, and steady advancement. Both are necessary, but it's important to use the correct method in the appropriate circumstances.

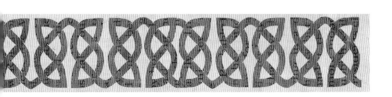

Chapter 5

The Significance of Trees and Mistletoe

All trees were sacred to the Celts. They provided so much—shelter, wood, nuts, and fruit, even medicines from bark and leaves. To the Druids, and hence to the Celts as a whole, they spanned the whole of existence, their roots deep under ground in the Otherworld, their sturdy trunks the solid foundations of the physical world, while their branches brushed the sky, reaching up to the heavens and the secrets of the celestial spheres. Slow-growing and patient (oak), fast-growing and supple (willow), or graceful and cheery (rowan), all had a place in the Celtic world, although some trees were more revered due to their practical uses or their deeper emotional and spiritual significance.

Oak

The mighty oak was particularly sacred to the Druids, who saw it as the prime example of the tree of life. The oak symbolized eternity. Its roots, sunk deep into the earth, are said to be as large and as great in extent as the mass of its wide spreading branches. Oaks grow slowly but surely and the wood is very strong and enduring, providing material for housing, tools, and fire. They can live for over a thousand years and grow to well over a hundred feet tall, giving rise to the saying "from little acorns mighty oaks do grow," suggesting that great achievements originate in small ideas.

Oaks tend to be struck by lightning more often than other trees, which may be partly due to the fact that the tree is one of the tallest, thereby presenting itself as more of a target than its shorter companions. It's also been suggested that the tree's physical makeup may make it something of a vegetable lightning rod. But whatever the reason may be, the oak has been associated with lightning and therefore with thunder, and hence with thunder and lightning gods, from time immemorial. It is said that oak leaves whisper ancient secrets to those who have the wit to understand, and its roots can lead you to knowledge of the Otherworld.

Oak symbolizes steady personal development and the accumulation of self-knowledge. It represents the ability to prevail against adversity, to acquire self-confidence as the result of learning how to deal with the circumstances life throws at us—and the steadiness to assimilate the occasional bolt of inspiration that can change our lives.

Birch

The graceful birch is one of life's pioneers, easily colonizing poor soil even in mountainous country. The silver variety was especially admired for its silvery bark, which can be used as a sort of paper, and the bright green leaves that appear in the spring and look almost like a mist from a distance, but all types of birch were held in high regard. It's said that Ogmios, the Celtic god of eloquence, wrote the first Ogham characters on a wand of birch wood. Traditionally, twigs and small branches of birch are used to make the besoms (brooms) that were used to sweep through the home, although whether this dates from Celtic times we can't say for sure because no evidence remains—wooden brooms would have rotted away, or been burnt once they had lost their usefulness. However, the pride the Celts took in appearance suggests that they probably did use something similar to a besom to keep the floors clean.

The sap of the birch is sweet, like the better-known maple, and can be tapped for use as a sweetener for food or to make an interesting variety of beer.

Birch symbolizes new beginnings, partly because it's one of the first trees to appear on newly cleared ground, and partly because its leaves appear very early in the spring.

Willow

The willow is one of the more versatile trees in the landscape. There are several different varieties—goat willow, crack willow, so called because its twigs break with a sharp cracking sound, and white willow. The latter two would have been most useful to the Celts. The bark of willows contains salicylic acid, an analgesic and the original source of the painkiller now known as aspirin. Chewed or steeped in hot water and drunk, the bitter-tasting substance is a very effective pain-reliever.

Usually found growing by water, willow is easy to grow. A broken twig pushed into the ground will often take root and swiftly develop into a new tree. White willow branches are particularly flexible, and can be woven into the baskets the Celts used for carrying harvested foodstuffs. The beauty of the wood is that it is tremendously supple when first cut and woven, but as it dries it hardens to produce a sturdy and resilient item. From simple round baskets to more complex artistic shapes, willow was the ideal medium for small household objects.

Given the speed at which it grows, willow was also useful for larger items, such as windbreaks, screens, and temporary hedging—to keep animals corralled close to the homestead during the winter, for example.

The willow bends with the wind, rather than standing against it and breaking. It teaches that a flexible mind and spirit will keep you from harm and heartbreak.

Apple

It seems plausible that the ancestors of all the many different apple varieties known today originated in the mountains of north-west China, the Himalayas, and Central Asia eons ago, gradually spreading into the rest of the world through the agency of migrating animals and their droppings. At the time, the fruit would have looked more like the crab apple than the fruit we know today. Small, crisp, and tart rather than sweet, it would have had a bright, clear taste, and been juicy and flavorful on the tongue.

Apples have the extraordinary quality of producing seedlings from their fruit that are quite different from the parent plant—which is no doubt a major reason for the vast number of varieties. To produce fruit identical to the parent tree, a branch of the original must be grafted on to a rootstock. But to have a seed produce something so different from the parent must have seemed magical to ancient peoples, and added to the fruit's mystique. Since earliest times the apple has been considered a magical fruit, a gift from the gods, a healthy, wholesome natural food that tasted wonderful, either raw or cooked. To some cultures it was the fruit of immortality, or of hidden knowledge—cut an apple in half crossways and you'll find a five-pointed star, the symbol of the pentagram and perceived by some as representing the perfected human being (see Samhain, page 17).

The fruit contains vitamin C and antioxidants, and its natural sugars are a source of energy. Apple trees are hardy, sturdy plants, able to grow in the north where other, softer fruit would perish. The tree is small, with gnarled branches and a wide-spreading crown. The scent of apple blossom is faint but beautiful, and not easily forgotten once experienced. The trees can't pollinate themselves, and rely on insects. Bees are probably the most common pollinators, and it's highly likely that hives would have been kept in the first orchards, and apple-blossom honey produced.

Over and above its usefulness as a food, however, to the Celts the apple symbolized the afterlife—Avalon, the Isle of Apples, where the sweet flowers grew on the same branches as the ripe fruit, and where there was no pain or distress, and everyone was forever young and happy. To some, Avalon may have been another name for Annwn, the Otherworld, separated from the mortal world by the thinnest of unseen barriers; to others it was the Blessed Isle, somewhere in Britain; to yet others it was an island away off the far west beyond the setting sun, to be reached only by dying, or by the living with the special dispensation and sailing skills of Manannan and his boat.

The apple tree and its fruit symbolize knowledge, especially mystical knowledge. The apple is very much a female symbol, associated with the female qualities of fertility, life-bearing, and nurturing. It represents the womb, eternity, heredity, and the continuance of the family in all its difference and diversity through the ages. It's a potent and powerful symbol for all women.

QUALITIES OF TREES

Alder sturdy and enduring

Ash robust and resilient

Aspen softness and humility

Beech versatile and helpful

Birch all-encompassing usefulness, health

Crab Apple fruitful and pretty

Hawthorn joyful celebration, spiritual protection

Hazel wisdom, serenity

Holly defense, physical protection

Hornbeam hard, remorseless

Juniper purification and prophecy

Lime straight and true

Oak staunch and dependable

Rowan magic, protection from enchantment and bad weather

Scots Pine nobility and leadership

Strawberry Tree welcoming and companionable

Willow supple and yearning

Yew stern, ruthless, and vigilant

Mistletoe

Mistletoe is a parasitic plant that grows on trees and shrubs, usually with no obvious ill-effects to a well-grown and sturdy tree. The seed, carried in birds' droppings, sticks to a branch, sending out a small tendril that penetrates the bark and takes root. Related parasitic plants have been given the same name but the original is a native of Celtic lands.

The Druids were reputed to use mistletoe as a medicine for bronchial complaints, barrenness, and perhaps as an antidote to poison, although mistletoe itself can be poisonous if too much is ingested. The plant was sacred to the Celts, especially if found growing on an oak or apple tree. Mistletoe appears as if by magic, growing high above the ground with nothing rooting it in the earth. Its seeds produce a white, viscous liquid with a distinct resemblance to semen, which led to it being perceived—either literally or metaphorically—as the seed of the gods. The branches and the leathery leaves point in two different directions from a single site, and to the Celts this symbolized the possibility of choice.

It was considered very unlucky to allow mistletoe to touch the ground. When cut, ceremoniously and reputedly with a golden sickle, it had to be caught before it dropped to the earth, preferably in a pure white cloth. It could then be used to make medicaments, or as talismans for protection.

Mistletoe symbolizes the ability to make rational choices, to direct your life as you desire, rather than being swept along by events. It represents male fertility, which is probably the origin of the tradition of kissing under the mistletoe—it asks for the blessings of the gods in matters of love.

Chapter 6

Animal Guides

Many animals were revered by the Celts for their innate qualities and virtues, and a number of them were associated with a particular deity. The animals that shared the land with humans were an integral part of the landscape, and thus sacred to the Great Mother, although Celtic pragmatism applied in this as in all things—animals provided useful food as a gift of the goddess, not to mention other bounties such as milk, wool, leather, and horn, to mention just a few.

Animals are represented in the heavens by constellations. Some of these are ancient, dating from prehistoric times, and would have been familiar to the Celts in their dealings with other cultures, while others are more modern, usually devised in the seventeenth century. Both are valid representations—to the Celts life involved change, growth, and development, the discovery of the new, or the rediscovery of the old.

By thinking about a chosen animal's qualities, we can often find inspiration on how to respond to events in our own lives. This can lead to powerful new insights and even changes of behavior. The shape of the animal, on jewelry say, can be a talisman, a reminder of a particular quality we admire and would like to encourage in ourselves.

Cow and Bull

Cattle were the staple symbol of wealth for the Celts, and were very highly prized: the larger the herd, the higher the status of its owner. When one chief or lord wished to challenge another, it was often accomplished by a cattle raid, in which warriors from one tribe would attempt to steal the cattle from a rival. To succeed without hindrance—and to keep the cattle once stolen—demonstrated the rival chief's lack of fitness to rule and could lead to his being replaced by someone more capable.

The Celts used milk for drinking and for making cream, cheese, and butter. They ate the meat and added the fat to stews to provide extra flavor and nourishment, and broke the bones to extract the marrow. The hide provided leather for shoes and other items. The horns were made into drinking vessels. Even the blood was used—as a libation to the land for fruitfulness and good crops. Cattle were also harnessed to the plough and used to help till fields.

The cattle kept by the Celts are likely to have been fairly small, sturdy, and shaggy, resembling Highland Cow or black Kerry cattle rather than the big, short-haired and variously colored breeds we know today. Cattle require a lot of pasture on which to graze, and were more prevalent among upland communities—or, at least, communities with access to moorland and heath.

Cows are usually fairly placid creatures, while bulls can be more aggressive, especially if annoyed. In Celtic times, bulls in particular were admired for their strength and virility, and the word is still used to refer to a particular type of man (even if it carries with it the implication of less than brilliant intellect!). In the heavens, the well-known and very ancient constellation of Taurus represents the bull, the prominent horns the proof of his virility.

Cattle symbolize plenty, wealth, and the hospitality of the feast, and were sacred to the Great Mother. As guides, the cow represents motherhood, nurturing, and patience, the bull short-tempered aggression, stamina, and vigor.

Wild Boar

The native wild pig used to be widespread in many parts of the UK, until it was wiped out by hunting and habitat destruction during the seventeenth century. It is making a small comeback in the UK—several small colonies have developed from farm escapees in the central part of the country. In Europe it is still fairly common throughout what were the Celtic lands.

The Celts respected the boar for its stubborn, indomitable ferocity, and adopted it as a symbol of war. At the same time it was a symbol of fertility and prosperity, fertility because of the number of piglets in a litter—four to six, and a roughly equal number of males and females—and prosperity because pork was very highly prized. The boar was one of the few animals to appear on

Celtic coinage. Wild boar took a considerable effort to hunt and catch, and the hunters needed to be highly skilled to be successful. Boars would continue to charge even when badly speared, and were quite capable of killing the hunter before dying themselves. Hence the development of the boar-spear, which has a sturdy cross piece behind the blade to prevent the boar from pushing itself further up the spear's shaft and attacking the human wielding it.

Boars symbolize the potential of the human spirit for righteous anger, for defense of the self and loved ones from threats. As a guide, the boar can give us the strength and confidence to stand up for what we know is right when threatened, and to use our anger constructively.

Otter

Once widespread along the waterways and coastal regions of Celtic lands, the Old World otter died out in many places as recently as the twentieth century. At home in the water, and surprisingly fast and agile on land, otters are alert, intelligent, curious, and most notably *playful* beings. Adults and children alike enjoy sliding—on snow, grass, or mud—and playing games of tag in and out of the water. The collective term, a romp of otters, is appropriate.

As a guide, the otter symbolizes light-heartedness, a childlike playfulness, and a joy in life that is redolent of summer days and glittering streams or frosty breath and snowball fights. It symbolizes the ability to slip in and out of the realms of the imagination and the physical world, and so represents the archetypal child within us all, regardless of

our circumstances or how deeply that child is hidden under layers of sophistication or pain. Follow the otter, diving deep into your self, and rediscover life's shining enchantment.

Horse

The horse was revered by the Celts, whose warriors were superlative horsemen whether riding the animal or using it to pull a chariot in battle. It was treated with great honor as a representative of the goddess, the deity who sustained the lives of all who lived upon her, in her particular incarnation of Epona, the goddess of the horse.

Highly intelligent animals, horses are fast and powerful, and while some can be a challenge to train, they are generally loyal and tractable. Each horse has its own character and temperament, and if the rider understands this and treats the horse sensitively, the relationship between horse and owner can be close and interdependent.

Horses have held a special place in the human psyche throughout history. They've appeared in prehistoric wall paintings, been transformed into centaurs, given wings to carry prophets and heroes, and in some cultures even been granted a horn to become the fabled unicorn. In the sky the horse is represented by the constellation of Pegasus, the winged horse of Greek mythology.

The horse is an ideal guide for the traveler. Sure-footed and enduring, the horse will carry us safely, leaving us free to save our energy and look around. The horse is the embodiment of nobility, freedom, and graceful motion. It does not fight for territory or dominance, but respects others according to their age, and holds ancestors in high regard.

Wolf

Humans have been both drawn to and repelled by the wolf throughout their mutual existence. The wolf is an intelligent and highly organized predator, working in packs to hunt and bring down prey—in which activity the earliest humans may have seen a reflection of their own methods of communal hunting. The wolf is also remorseless, driven by its need for food for itself and its young to hunt any animal, wild, domesticated, or two-legged if necessary.

At the same time it's a beautiful, graceful, and seemingly loving creature, as anyone who has seen adults and cubs together will attest. Wolves live in a close-knit pack of up to twenty animals, most of them related, with a strict hierarchy. The pack leaders are known as the alpha male and female; generally the alpha male governs the dog-wolves and the alpha female the bitches. The "top" alpha governs the whole pack—and it's usually the alpha female. The other wolves "fight" for position within the pack, such fights also keeping them in fit condition for the trials that life brings.

Wolves are built for speed and stamina. Powerful legs and paws adapted to handle almost any terrain, and an excellent sense of smell, make them superb hunters. Their prey in Celtic times would have included deer, beavers, foxes, and other small mammals. Sheep and goats are easy prey for them, hence the unease with which they were viewed by livestock owners. Yet wolves helped to maintain the natural balance, keeping down the numbers of animals that could become pests if allowed to breed unrestricted—a balance that wasn't fully understood until recently, after the damage was done and the wolf had been wiped out across huge swathes of the globe.

With its thick, soft-looking gray fur and golden eyes that seem to sparkle with intelligence, the wolf appeals to something deep within the human spirit—a feeling of distant kinship, perhaps, or a desire to run with the wolf through

ancient forests under the moon. It's an echo of a simpler, if more savage time. Our veneer of civilization is thin, despite the trappings of Western culture and our belief in our own sophistication.

The wolf guides us to an understanding of the primitive side of our nature, that part of us that yearns for acceptance into the pack and the exhilaration of the hunt—the awareness of strength in numbers, and that the survival of the pack is all-important. It symbolizes the urge to nurture and protect the young, the future of our species. And it may also symbolize the outcast, the lone survivor of the death of the pack, and the search for a mate. Wolf teaches that you will flourish only if you are yourself, untamed and unbowed. He knows himself, his strengths and weaknesses, and he works for mutual benefit, taking only what he needs—no more, no less.

Stag

The red deer, native to the UK and Europe, was a familiar sight to the Celts. Adapted to life in woodland, it would have been perfectly at home in the vast forests that once covered the land. The stags are famed for their magnificent antlers—spreading bony outgrowths from the skull, covered by a soft layer of "velvet" until the bone hardens. These are shed and regrown every year.

The Celts hunted deer for their meat and for their antlers, which were often used to make the handles of weapons, talismanically conferring the strength and skill of the stag on the weapon just as the meat would have transferred health and strength to the person eating it. A large deer could feed a small Celtic community for several days, and would have been viewed as a blessing from Cernunnos as well as a tribute to the skills of the hunters who caught the animal.

The stag is a powerful creature, fast and strong, and capable of considerable ferocity when defending his own. He symbolizes Cernunnos (Herne), the antler-crowned Lord of the Hunt and god of all animals.

Noble and graceful, the stag embodies strength and stamina. More than any other animal except the fox, the stag can act as a guide into the heart of our personal Wildwood (see page 137), the great primal forest that exists deep within each of us. The stag knows all the paths—and where there is no path, he will make one. You may have difficulty keeping up with him—he is sure of himself, and unwilling to wait for stragglers—but if you trust to your own half-forgotten instincts, you will be able to follow him, or use the paths he has provided.

Walking with the stag, letting him show you the secret places of your mind, is a rare and wonderful experience. The stag can be both defensive and aggressive, fleeing from danger or standing his ground—especially if someone tries to encroach on what he views as his property. He instinctively knows which is the correct action to take.

Hound

No one knows for certain when humans first started taming wolves—it happened before recorded history, and estimates vary from 100,000 to 15,000 years ago in what is now China. It's possible that during cold winters wolves were drawn to human camps by the lure of food and warmth, and gradually became used to humans. A symbiotic relationship would have built up, wolves helping with the hunt and guarding camps in return for food and shelter.

Over time the fastest and friendliest domesticated wolves would have been bred together, and gradually the ancestors of the dog varieties we know today would have developed. The breeding of particular hounds for specific types of hunting is an ancient practice, employed in Egypt, Greece, and Rome—and undoubtedly by the Celts.

Celtic hounds were used mainly for hunting, at least initially. When the culture became mainly agrarian, dogs began to be used to guard livestock and the general community—and some may even have been kept as pets. There are a number of statues showing a representation the Great Mother accompanied by a small hound, or with a small dog sitting on her lap. Certainly the smaller dogs may well have been trained to look after babies and young children in the home. In the British Isles this smaller dog may have been the ancestor of what later became the Welsh Corgi, believed to have been brought into the country from the area around the Black Sea at the end of the second millennium BCE.

Hounds bred for the hunt, however, were usually large. The breeds we know today as the Deerhound, the Wolfhound (called *Cú Faoil* by Irish Celts), and the now rare Otterhound were bred to hunt the animals indicated by their names. In Britain, the Deerhound was used to hunt red deer specifically, being very fast and big enough to pull one down, after which the human hunters would despatch it swiftly. Its close relative the Wolfhound was employed in the hunting of boars as well as wolves.

The Celts regarded their hounds very highly. It was considered an honor for a warrior to be compared to one. Cúchulain—the Hound of Culain—never changed his name back to the one he was given at birth, and Cunobelinus—Hound of Belenus—was one of the most famous of the pre-Roman British kings. Shakespeare wrote a play about him, *The Tragedy of Cymbeline, King of Britain*.

Dogs are now so common and useful in daily life that we tend to forget where they came from and their original purposes. Whether assisting blind or deaf people to lead an independent life, helping the police or mountain rescue teams, herding sheep or cattle, guarding our homes or valuables, or simply providing living playmates for our children and ourselves, the lives of the descendants of those ancient hounds are closely entwined with our own. Life would be much poorer without them.

In the heavens, the ancient constellations of Canis Major and Canis Minor, the large and small hunting dogs not far from Orion, recall the importance of the hound to ancient peoples. Sirius, the brightest star in the sky after the sun, forms the heart of Canis Major. It could be seen in the pre-dawn sky just before the summer solstice, making it an important calendar marker and of particular interest to the Druids, who were learned in celestial lore.

Devotion, active protection, and companionship are the hound's areas. It's an appropriate guide for everyone, especially young people and those who live alone.

Bear

As the human population increased and the natural forests decreased, the great bear slowly became less and less widespread through Celtic lands, until it died out in a great many places. There are none left in Britain, yet such is the powerful appeal of the creature that even today it is associated with nobility. Due to its great size, strength, cunning, adaptability, and its ability to stand upright on its hind legs and thus tower over everyone in its vicinity, the bear symbolized power and kingship in ancient times. The legendary Arthur was named for the bear—artos.

Bears hold a special place in our consciousness. The ancient constellations of Ursa Major and Ursa Minor—the Big and Little Bears—are circumpolar and used not only to find north, but as pointers to many other stars, which would have made them very familiar and useful in Druidic skylore. The two celestial bears, circling around the fixed point of the Polaris northern star at the end of the bear cub's tail, provided a stable reference point for everyone at night, especially during the cold, clear nights of winter. (The slight wobble in the earth's orbit known as precession means that Polaris hasn't always been the pole star—even now it's a degree away from true north.)

As a guide, the bear symbolizes wisdom and dedication. Bear is an ideal talisman for anyone following a course of study, as it urges Druidic focus and concentration. The bear was known for its good memory, able to find its way back to previously discovered sites of good hunting or feeding. It was also a fearless explorer. A bear guide may lead you safely into unfamiliar and fruitful territory. Bear also encourages creativity by thoughtful withdrawal, whether in meditation or retreat.

Crow and Raven

Crows and ravens are opportunistic carrion feeders, eating flesh that has already been killed. Along with their black plumage and harsh cawing cry, this has given them a dark reputation as omens of death and destruction, whereas they are among the most intelligent of birds, their intellect apparently on a par with dolphins and wolves in the animal world.

Myths of crows and ravens are almost universal, from the ravens Thought and Memory, who perched on Odin's shoulders and advised him in council, to the Hindu god Sani, who rides a crow. To the Celts they were the Morrigan's birds, symbolizing her as the bringer of death on the battlefield. To see them hovering predicted bloodshed in the near future. Yet the crow and the raven serve a useful purpose, helping to clear the ground of the destruction wrought by men, and, by extension, leaving it prepared for new growth. In this guise they symbolize the cycle of life-death-rebirth in its most forceful, dynamic form.

Their other role is as prophet and messenger from the Otherworld. These aren't always messages of death and doom. Ravens warned Llugh of his enemies' approach, so that he could prepare for their attack, and two "druidic ravens" announced Cúchulain's presence on his quest to assist the sea goddess Fand against her enemies.

As guides, crow and raven are not for the faint hearted. They may lead you into uncomfortable territory. You must accept your own mortality before you can ponder what may happen after death. More importantly, they lead you to consider if your life has taken the most fulfilling path. Do you need to make changes? They waste nothing, and urge us to do the same.

Snake

There weren't many varieties of snake in northern Celtic lands—most of these reptiles, being cold-blooded, prefer warmer climes. Several types of venomous viper, the harmless grass snake, and the non-venomous smooth snake were, and are still, to be found and of these, the European viper and the largest species of grass snake are the only ones native to the UK. The viper—also called the adder in the UK—is the most cold-tolerant snake in the northern hemisphere. All these snakes are generally shy creatures and will strike only if threatened. Most bites happen when someone accidentally disturbs or steps on the snake.

When hunting, the adder injects venom into its prey and then moves back, following by scent until the animal collapses. This strategy allows it to avoid being hurt by the animal fighting back or struggling. It eats amphibians, lizards, nestlings, and small mammals, all of which can inflict damage in a battle for survival. Adders hibernate, often communally and under logs, from September to March. They breed in April and May, and the females give live birth in August, which is unusual as most snakes lay eggs, but which makes good sense given the colder weather in the North.

The grass snake is completely harmless, its defense mechanisms being first to swell up and hiss loudly. If this has no effect, it will produce a vile-smelling liquid, and if this doesn't repel the threat, finally it will feign death.

GUIDE TO RADICAL CHANGE

As a guide, the snake—complex and extraordinarily powerful—always signifies transformation. It is associated with physical sexuality, seduction, and sexual power, both male and female, but it also symbolizes the ability to slough off old habits and attitudes, leaving the mind clear to learn new truths. On yet another level the snake symbolizes hidden wisdom and secrets, the ability to draw on inner, sometimes instinctive or spiritual knowledge. It encompasses the full range of human experience, belief and desire, and the three regions—the Otherworld, the sacred land, and the heavens—and the flow of life energy between them. Snake tells us that everything is connected and making changes in one area affects all others.

Before taking snake as a guide, it's important to understand that any changes brought about under its guidance will have far-reaching consequences. They will be profound, life-changing—and irreversible. If you are happy with your life as it is, or you're afraid of change, snake isn't the guide for you. If you choose snake—or if snake chooses you—a sense of personal responsibility is necessary. You will no longer be able to blame others for your success or failure in life. But such successes are very sweet, and our failures teach us where we went wrong, so that next time we can act in a different way. Secure in snake's coils, decide how to make the changes necessary to transform yourself into the person you really want to be.

Snakes have always been seen as mysterious creatures, supple enough to tie themselves in knots yet able to move amazingly swiftly over the ground or in water, despite having no legs. The finding of sloughed snake-skin may have led to a belief that snakes were immortal, simply shedding their old body when it wore out rather than dying. Later the snake came to symbolize hidden or occult knowledge, the power of transformation and rebirth. It also symbolizes healing, and is still seen on the caduceus, the staff used to represent the medical profession.

The snake's return to the world in the spring, from burrows in the ground, linked it to the Otherworld and the wisdom that came from the gods.

Owl

Solitary, mainly nocturnal hunters, owls are often linked with death and adversity, yet they are truly amazing birds. Perfectly adapted to night-hunting, their flight feathers have soft, fluffy edges, which gives them near-silent flight. Their vision is superb at long-distance, but poor at close quarters, making them unable to see things in front of their faces. They have a distinctive appearance, with large, front-facing, usually golden eyes and a small sharp beak in a facial disc that gives the face a faint resemblance to a flower. They can turn their heads more than 120 degrees in both directions, enabling them to look behind them with ease. Owls' hearing is acute at certain frequencies, and some have asymmetrically placed ears, one being higher and a little further back than the other, allowing them to pinpoint their prey with amazing accuracy. The facial disc acts a little like radar, directing minute sounds into the ears, where the tiny differences in the time each sound takes to reach each ear allows for precise detection of the prey.

Owls have dual symbolism. Some cultures view them as harbingers of misfortune, but others see them as wise birds, imbued with hidden knowledge and occult learning. Although the legend of Blodeuwedd, the flower maiden turned into an owl as punishment for loving a man other than her husband (see page 52), seems very negative, in fact Gwydion may have done her a favor. The owl directs its own destiny while Blodeuedd had no control over her fate. The owl has few predators, although crows may attack ferociously should they ever encounter a wakeful owl in daylight. This hostility could be interpreted on a totemic level as a dichotomy between hidden knowledge, represented by the owl, and open prophecy, symbolized by the crow—or perhaps it's natural antipathy between the silent, solitary hunter of the night and the noisy crowd of carrion-eaters.

The owl is an appropriate guide for those who work alone, often late into the night—the self-employed, the artist and writer, the explorer in any field, and those entrusted with secrets. It urges alertness and awareness of our surroundings, whether physical or mental. With owl as your guide, trust your own intuition to allow you to detect the hidden agendas of others.

Salmon

Salmon are fast and powerful—they have to be to swim against river currents—and can grow up to five feet in length. However, they will thrive only where water quality is high—the presence of salmon in a river is reliable evidence of the watersource's health.

To the Celts, a fish that can live in both fresh and salt water—one that straddles both "worlds"—would have been seen as something very special, and the salmon is present in several Celtic legends and tales. It always symbolizes wisdom and advancement. In the Irish Fenian Cycle the fish had eaten nine hazel nuts that had fallen into the Fountain of Wisdom from the nine hazel trees surrounding the water, and thus gained all the knowledge of the world. The first person to eat its flesh would gain the same wisdom. The bard Finn Eces had been hunting the salmon for seven years, but was unable to catch it until taking on the young hero Fionn mac Cumhaill as apprentice. Fionn was set to watch the fish cooking, but burned his thumb on its skin. Putting his thumb into his mouth to ease the burn, he inadvertently tasted the salmon and gained all the wisdom that Finn Eces had intended for himself. Ever after, if he was presented with a difficult problem, all he had to do was suck his thumb while thinking and the answer would come to him.

There's a parallel in the tale of Taliesin's birth, where the young servant Gwion accidentally tastes the potion Ceridwen is making for her son, Avaggdu, and thus gains all the wisdom and knowledge intended for him. Knowing Ceridwen would be furiously angry with him, Gwion runs away (see page 53). One of the creatures he becomes in his attempts to escape is a fish. Later, after Gwion is reborn, Ceridwen places the baby into a leather bag and throws him into the ocean. Elphin of Ceredigion catches the bag instead of the salmon for which he is fishing, and cares for and raises the baby, whom he names Taliesin ("radiant brow").

Cúchulain's most famous action is the "salmon leap," which brought him down upon his enemies from above. It may also be how he crossed the Bridge of Leaps to reach the home of the Scáthach, the Druidess who taught him the arts of war.

When Kai and Gwrhyr were searching for Mabon (see page 36), they asked a series of animals, each one wiser than the last, where he was imprisoned. The last of them was the wisest and oldest creature alive, the salmon of Llyn Llyw, who took the two heroes on his back to the dungeon where the Divine Child was being held.

The salmon symbolizes wisdom, both pure knowledge and wisdom in action, and can hardly be bettered as a talisman and guide for everyone.

Swan

The swan was the largest bird known to the Celts, and the mute swan would have been the most familiar to them.

A wealth of legend and myth surround swans, from almost everywhere in the world. In Celtic legend, Lir was the father of Manawydan, the god of the sea. As well as his famous son, Lir and his wife, Aeb, had four other children. After Aeb's death, the motherless children were unhappy, and Lir took another wife, Aoife. Aoife, however, grew jealous of the children, and on a journey to visit her father with the children, ordered the people of the Lake of the Oaks to kill them. They refused, so, lacking the courage to do the deed herself, she transformed them into swans, linked to each other by a golden chain, and put a curse on them so that they should remain in that guise for 900 years. (For this dreadful deed Dearg the King transformed Aoife into an air-demon.) The children of Lir retained their human voices, however, and sang so sweetly that all who heard them were enchanted. When they were finally returned to human form, they immediately withered into old men and woman and died.

Their tale is a tragic one, yet it has an element of beauty about it. Although condemned to live as swans, nevertheless the children had long and peaceful lives, as the king had decreed that no swan should ever be killed, in case it was one of the children—and as the daughter Fionnuala said to her stepmother, their minds were free, even if their bodies were trapped.

The cloaks of the Druids and Bards are reputed to have been made of feathers, the swan's among them. In the sky, the swan is represented by the constellation of Cygnus, wings outstretched in flight.

Like wolves, swans usually mate for life. Courting swans "dance" on the water, their necks and heads making the heart shape that we associate so intimately with romance. On the water the bird embodies elegance—they are less graceful on land—and beauty, and in some traditions have been used to represent the soul. The myth that it is silent until just before it dies is appealing but untrue. The swan makes a loud hissing noise to frighten off anyone intruding into its territory—and it can't sing at all.

As a guide, the swan fosters self-assurance and the ability to face problems with grace and serenity, no matter what life throws at us. The swan teaches that everyone carries the potential for a radiant and everlasting beauty of mind and spirit, and that exterior appearance, which will change and fade with the passing years, is of lesser importance. It's an excellent guide for anyone lacking self-confidence, and inspires us to greater efforts to achieve our goals.

Hawk and Falcon

Taxonomically hawks and falcons belong to different families, but a variety of different species would have been recognized by the Celts, from the hovering kestrel to the shrub-skimming sparrowhawk. All are smallish birds of prey, fast and possessed of superb eyesight.

As a guide, the hawk or falcon symbolizes clear-sightedness and speed, the ability to look ahead, consider consequences and act upon them quickly. It's a good guide for those in business or involved in politics, but its qualities should not be misused, or it may lead into danger.

Eagle

The sight of a magnificent golden eagle, with its huge wingspan—more than six feet in the adult—would have been almost as unusual in Celtic times as it is now. The bird naturally prefers treeless terrain, moorland, and mountain, and is extremely sensitive to disturbance. Nests are generally built in inaccessible places, and usually just one chick, out of the one to three eggs laid and hatched, survives.

Lleu Llaw Gyffes, son of the moon deity Arianrhod, fled from Blodeuwedd and her lover in the form of an eagle, until Gwydion the magician restored him to human form. There is an association between the eagle and the sun—both are golden in color and seen high in the sky. And, if only because of its size and magnificence, it's likely that the eagle was regarded by the Druids as sacred. In the heavens the Eagle is represented by the constellation of Aquila, which straddles the bright band of the Milky Way.

Splendid isolation, lordship, and the loneliness that comes with being at the top are the Golden Eagle's territory. As well as bestowing a determination to survive, golden eagle acts as a reminder that you still need the basic necessities, and the goodwill of others, to thrive.

Dove

Evidence that the dove was around in Celtic times is to be found on contemporary statuary. Doves and pigeons would have provided a good source of food for the Celts—they are not particularly speedy birds, and can be trapped fairly easily. The taste and high protein value of the meat would have made it worth the effort of plucking.

The white dove, however, was viewed a little differently. Its pure white plumage marked it as special—white animals were sacred to the Druids in particular, but the white dove's gleaming plumage and gentle cooing voice, especially in the mating season, appeals to everyone.

The doves' courtship ritual involves the male "dancing" to attract the female, spreading his wings and cooing at her as he ducks his head and struts in a circle around her. It's a pretty display, and although in truth it's simply a biologically impelled method of attracting her attention, humans tend to assign human characteristics to animals. From ancient times the courtship of white doves symbolized the love between two people. Doves were sacred to Venus, the Roman goddess of love. Releasing a pair of white doves to fly free is a delightful way to celebrate a loving union.

As a guide, the dove symbolizes gentleness and reconciliation, romance and the tranquility of a warm and steady love. It's an ideal talisman for lovers, especially for those in a long-term committed relationship, acting as a reminder to re-affirm their love and let each other know how special they are. Sometimes we forget what made us fall in love in the first place, and take the other for granted. The dove reminds us that love is a precious thing, worth protecting.

Hare

Hares are shy creatures, except during the mating season in the spring, when they can be seen racing around over open country, or standing up on their hind legs "boxing" each other with their forepaws. At one time such a fight was thought to be between two males (known as jacks) competing for a female (the jill), but evidence now suggests that a female may hare-box with a male, either to indicate her unreadiness for mating, or possibly to test how fit he might be as a mate.

The original Easter Bunny was a hare, and the association of hares and eggs may come from a thirteenth-century tradition. It was said that farmers ploughing fields often came across clutches of eggs in the grass, erroneously believing them to be hare eggs. Of course, both the hare and eggs are symbolic of fertility, and intimately associated with the Great Mother, and the notion of hares being born from eggs is probably very much older than the thirteenth century.

The symbol of three hares running in a circle and joined at the ears has been found all the way from the South West of England, through Europe and the Middle East, to India. This is believed to be a lunar symbol, and because the moon is often considered to be female, it may also represent the three stages of female life—youth, maturity, and old age. It tell us that the cycle of life is unending; the hares chase each other unceasingly in an elegant and infinitely reassuring image.

In the heavens, the constellation of Lepus the hare sits below the feet of Orion the hunter.

Hare is another challenging guide, and unsuitable for anyone lacking self-confidence or a sense of groundedness. The hare may lead you zigzagging down strange and novel paths, showing you aspects of yourself you didn't know existed and might find disturbing. On the other hand, if you need to be nimble-minded to deal with day-to-day matters, hare may serve your purposes well. Talismanically, the hare may be helpful anywhere fast thinking or fast action is required. It counsels against getting pulled down by worries that tie you to the past.

Fox

Renowned as a sly, wily, and intelligent animal, the fox is hugely adaptable. From the sandy-colored big-eared desert fox to the white thick-furred, small-eared, and tough Arctic fox, this small mammal has found a niche in almost every environment, including modern cities.

Foxes are normally shy and wary of humans. They mate in late December, which links them with the Yule festival and the turning of the year. The astonishingly human-sounding scream of the vixen would have made the forest even more frightening than usual in Celtic times.

In legend the fox has a variable reputation. It can represent cunning and trickery, but is also often seen as a helpful creature. To the Celts it would most likely have symbolized the autumn and the cooling of the year, its copper-red fur a reflection of the falling leaves and the lowering sun. Its wary nature would make it seem very much a manifestation of the spirit of the Wildwood—and possibly a messenger from humans to Cernunnos, the Lord of the Forest. Its celestial counterpart, the faint constellation Vulpecula (the little fox), is not of Celtic origin—it was devised in the seventeenth century. It can be found between Cygnus the swan and Aquila the eagle.

The fox symbolizes adaptability and the wisdom to know how to use it to best advantage. Fox's occasional mischievous inclination urges us not to let fear overwhelm our sense of natural wonder. The fox embraces opportunities and thrives as a result.

Badger

The sturdy badger with its distinctive black and white striped face would have been very familiar to the Celts. Large and fairly weighty, the badger is primarily a nocturnal creature, emerging from its communal sett at twilight to feed. The sett can contain over ten individual badgers, sows, and boars, living together as a clan. A separate nesting chamber for pregnant females leads off the main area. It seems likely that setts are handed down from generation to generation, enlarged as necessary, and made comfortable with dried grasses and bracken.

Badgers have a thick pelt, stocky frame, and extremely powerful legs. As digging animals, their claws are short but very strong, and can cause real damage when used for defense. Badger cubs are renowned for their playfulness.

Badgers are considered wise, courageous, noble, and long-suffering. As a guide, badger symbolizes the ability to dig in, retrench and hold our position, passively and quietly resisting being forced into situations against our will. Badger also reminds us of the value of play to release mental tension.

Beaver

Widespread throughout Celtic lands, beavers keep waterways clear of debris and help all aquatic creatures to prosper. The beaver's broad flattened tail is used as a rudder while swimming, and also to give a warning signal if danger approaches. The sharp "slap" of a beaver's tail on the water's surface is a sound that carries a long way, both above and below water. The animals are quite dextrous, being able to hold objects in their front paws; their hindpaws are webbed, making them speedy underwater. They are probably best known for their habit of felling trees and building dams to create pools, to provide easier access to food in the winter, and for protection. In Europe, beavers tend to live in burrows in the riverbank with the entrance below the waterline, like otters, but they will also build a home, known as a lodge, in the center of the pools they create. This is usually a two-chambered dwelling with an underwater entrance to keep other animals out.

The pools provide benefits for many other creatures as well. They encourage the increase of aquatic insects and amphibians, such as frogs and newts, and hence fish and birds, which in turn provide food for otters and wading birds such as the heron—and, in the past, the human hunter and fisher. Beavers tend to feed and fell trees close to the water's edge, thus clearing the ground for new growth. Low undergrowth on the riverbank allows sunlight to reach water plants, which may not happen if the water is overhung by branches. The cleared areas also create grazing opportunities for larger animals, such as deer. As the water slowly spreads behind the dam, it helps create natural wetland, one of the richest environments in nature. The dams can help control flooding as well, by slowing the force of the water.

Beavers are very sociable animals, living in family groups that to some extent echo that of a small human family. A male and female, with their near-adult children, yearlings, and the current year's kits, live together in lodge or burrow, sharing the work of building or repairing the dam, hunting, feeding, and relaxing together, grooming and looking after the infants.

The beaver symbolizes industry and family co-operation. Its ability to alter the landscape for its own purposes while nevertheless improving it for everything else, makes it a good role model for anyone wishing to live in harmony with the natural world while still retaining their home comforts. As a guide the beaver counsels hard work, teamwork, and diligence, and the building of useful systems to make life easier.

RESPECT FOR ANIMALS

The Celts hunted animals for food. Today very few of us need or desire to hunt, and those who do mostly do so for "sport." It goes without saying that deliberately inflicting needless pain, physical or mental, on any of the Great Mother's children is to be avoided wherever possible. Fox-hunting, deer hunting for anything other than an environmentally necessary cull, cock-fighting, or the appallingly cruel badger baiting are not pursuits that the genuine seeker of ancient wisdom should tolerate or support.

Chapter 7

The Sacred Landscape

To the Celts the land itself was sacred, the embodiment of the Mother Goddess, who sustained and supported them. The Celts belonged to her as much as she did to them. Life flowed through her hills and rivers and her bounty fed the creatures living in and upon her body. Each hill and valley, each grove and cave, had a life, a spirit, a *genius loci* of its own—and often its own native deity. The Great Mother was loved and deeply respected, and no Celt would dream of harming her.

The fortunes of the king and the land were bound together. When chosen by the Druids, the king or chief was symbolically wedded to the land, and his actions thereafter intimately linked to the land's fertility. If he subsequently failed in his duties and the land suffered because of it, he could be deposed and replaced. It was an equitable and practical system. No doubt the knowledge that they would be replaced if they failed in their duties persuaded many rulers to act wisely rather than being tempted to abuse their power and position.

Lessons to Take Away

The concept of the land and all it means is still overwhelmingly powerful today. Wars are fought over it, exiles try to reshape their surroundings to resemble it, people struggle and impoverish themselves to own a little of it, others swear allegiance to it and die in its defense. Our motherland is still as vital a part of us today as it was to the Celts, even if we may not fully recognize the fact. We instinctively identify with the place we consider to be our native land, although it may not be the place where we were born and raised, and to be exiled from it, even by our own agency, can leave us feeling lost and rootless.

But the concept of the land can be more than simply a physical place. It can also symbolize a place within ourselves, in our psyche or spirit, a place of safety to which we can withdraw in times of distress. It can represent the ground from which our qualities and virtues spring, our innermost selves. Of course, by itself the land can't produce much—it needs sunlight and rainwater to be productive, to bring forth the living bounty that hides just below the surface. And deeper down lie great treasures—precious metals and jewels, the roots of springs, the entrances into the mysteries of the Otherworld—our minds.

The Three Worlds

The number three was revered by the Celts. It symbolized their three "worlds"—the Otherworld of spirits and deities, the mortal world, and the celestial sphere from which came sunshine and rain to nourish the land, the moon to mark the months, and the stars by whose configuration night-time direction-finding was possible. The Great Mother was a triple goddess, her three forms separate but still blending into one powerful whole. We still find three an especially satisfying number. It symbolizes stability and wholeness, the complete being of body, mind, and spirit, the realms of earth, sea, and sky, the traditional categories of animal, mineral, and vegetable, good—and bad—things "coming in threes." The concept of three has an ancient and venerable history and it's comforting to think that the Celts appreciated the number just as much as we do.

TRISKELE   TRIQUETA

Two of the Celts' most enduring and important symbols are based on the number three, the triqueta and the triskele. The triskele intimately symbolizes the threefold nature of life and the interconnectedness of all things. It resembles a complex labyrinth (see page 146) and its spiraling nature, drawn using only one line, evokes the act of breathing, or the blood cycling in the veins and arteries of the body. It may also represent the three times three months of pregnancy, linking it to the Great Mother.

The triqueta is similar, but where the triskele symbolizes outstretching infinity, the triqueta is a more contained symbol, its elements overlapping. It is defensive rather than expansive, protective rather than outward-looking. It contains all things within it, holds them safe rather than releasing them to find their own way. In the triqueta, the center represents the heart.

The Sky

What is above regulates what is below. The rising and setting of the sun to a regular yearly pattern allowed for crops to be sown and harvested at the right time. The clouds spoke of what weather was approaching—storm, rain, snow, or clear skies—and advised the people to take action accordingly. The appearance of certain constellations in the evening sky marked the start of certain seasons—Orion's evening rising saw the start of winter, for example— and allowed for navigation in the dark. The moon was highly significant, not only as a source of light at night, but as a marker for the months of the Celtic year. The Celts measured their day from sunset to sunset, suggesting that the features of the night sky were at least as important as the day—which would indeed be the case for hunters, as most of the game animals of the time tended to be more active at night. The five known planets—Mercury, Mars, Venus, Saturn, and Jupiter, all that could be seen by the naked eye—moved through the sky on regular paths that were noted and recorded. Various Roman writings record that the Druids spent much time in discourse on the stars and their motions, the scope of the universe and the nature of the physical world. They were philosophers as well as teachers, straddling the worlds of the real and measurable and the sacred and untouchable with ease.

Meteor showers would have fallen at regular times of the year, eclipses would have occasioned awe or alarm, and in the several millennia of the Celts' existence as a culture no doubt some comets appeared in the sky. It is likely that the Druids practiced a form of astrology, although we have no record of what form it might have taken, only hints in old Irish texts that mention its existence. The Celts who had trading contacts with other peoples would have known of the original Babylonian system and more than likely passed it on, since the Druids valued knowledge of all kinds. It's reasonable to assume that they used a variety of devices to help with their observations. A large number of megalithic structures marking the rising of the sun on the solstices and the movements of the moon, among other celestial phenomena, still remain across Celtic lands. Stonehenge and Avebury in England, the Callanish Standing Stones in the Hebrides, Bryn Celli Ddu in Wales, Newgrange in Ireland, and Carnac in Brittany are perhaps the best known. These great stone monuments predate the Celts, but the Druids may well have adopted them.

The sky symbolizes limitlessness, the outward-reaching human spirit and the yearning to explore, to push back boundaries. The beautiful blue arch above us represents the heights we can attain, free of the boundaries that constrain our lives.

The Sun—the Solar Wheel

The sun has always occupied a central role in all religions throughout the millennia, which is hardly surprising—a huge ball of fire in the sky, too bright to look at for any length of time without going blind, that provides the earth with warmth. Its presence makes the days pleasant, and it wouldn't have taken long for observant humans to associate the longer days and warmer weather of spring and summer with the appearance of new plants and the renewal of old ones after the hiatus of winter, thus linking the sun with growth, and with life itself.

For the Celts, the sun primarily regulated the natural world, the plants and animals on earth. The Light Year was a time of cheer, but also of hard work in preparation for the times when the sun rose low on the southern horizon and set again after only a few hours of pallid light and little warmth. Yet it was a comforting cycle, allowing for a slower pace in the Dark Year, a time to rest and catch one's breath.

Belenos/Lugh embodied the qualities of the sun, its life-giving and health-promoting virtues. The symbol is the solar wheel, an image of the ever-turning and cycling year that has appeared in different versions in different religions across the world, but finds its simplest form in the four- or eight-spoked wheel.

The sun symbolizes the cycles of the year, the regular patterns that control our lives. It represents the heart, the center around which all things revolve. Its specific meaning may be different for each of us. For some it may be our children, for others our partner, or our work, art, music, the environment, or a combination of factors blending together to make a harmonious whole. It is our own heart, those things that make our life bright and sweet, the center of our being, to be treasured and loved.

The Moon

The word month refers to one complete moon-phase cycle, often from new moon to new moon, although waxing crescent to waxing crescent is also possible. We don't know for certain which particular moon phase the Celts used to mark the beginning of the month, but since they marked the new day from sunset and the new year from beginning of winter, it's feasible that they started the month at the dark of the moon. Each month also consisted of a bright half—from new moon to full—and a dark half—from full moon to new again—a fact reflected in the term "fortnight," a contraction of the Old English words for fourteen nights.

Since the moon's orbit isn't a regular circle, additional days were added to make the "lunar year" (354 days) equal to the solar year (a little over 364 days). The Celtic Coligny Calendar, discovered in 1897, probably dates back to the first or second century CE although its sources may date from nearly a thousand years earlier. It shows how the Celts added an extra month every two and a half years or so, using calculations that worked on a thirty-year cycle.

The calendar was arranged in tables with small holes on each line of information, apparently so that pegs could be inserted, perhaps to mark forthcoming festivals. The astronomical knowledge, precise observation, and careful recording over decades in order to create such a complex device is compelling evidence for the sophistication of the Druids.

To the Celts, the phase of the moon was an immediate way of telling what day it was, in which fortnight. But this beautiful silver wheel in the heavens also gave light to brighten the night for much of the month, and its correlation with a woman's fertility cycle linked it with women's secret knowledge. The moon symbolizes the inevitable progression of time, female fertility, and the dreams that come with sleep. It always shows us one face, hiding the rest of itself in shadow. It represents the mysteries in life, the things we long to know that may never be revealed.

Annwn, Tir na nÓg, the Otherworld

To the Celts, the place one went to after death was both physical and a state of being. It was not a stable, fixed location, but could be underground, or far over the sea to the west, or it could be right beside the mortal world, separated by the thinnest of veils to confound the eyes of humans. It was the home of the gods and, temporarily, the spirits of those who had died, along with other beings whose names and forms are less clearly described, "fey folk," the spirits of the natural world, or possibly the spirits of ancestors who had chosen not to be reborn. To most Celts, it was a beautiful, serene, and happy place, always at the height of summer, where no one ever aged and where there was no pain, hunger, or thirst. Sometimes called the Isles of the Blessed, or Avalon, the Isle of Apples (see page 91), Tír na nÓg, the Land of Youth, and in more modern times referred to as the Summerlands, this mystical place could be entered by living mortals under certain conditions and at certain places.

Caves could be entrances to Annwn, as could cromlechs (see page 154) and burial mounds. Glastonbury in the south west of England was, and for many people still is, believed to be the original Avalon, and a place where one may enter Annwn. We cannot be sure of the precise location of the entrance—which in itself is a feature of the mystery of the Otherworld—but it was most likely somewhere on Glastonbury Tor. Traditionally, Glastonbury was reputed to be the site of a Druid university. It's an area rich in both history and legend, and combines a number of elements of great significance to the Celts.

Glastonbury Tor rises over 500 feet above the flood plain of the Somerset levels. In ancient times it would have floated above mist and flood waters like a green and fertile island. A seven-tiered labyrinth (see page 146) created on the slopes of the Tor formed a twisting, spiraling path up to the summit. It has been suggested that the Tor is Caer Sidi of Welsh legend. Glastonbury also features a spring reputed to have great healing powers, which flows into what is now called the Chalice Well.

An individual could be invited to visit Annwn by one of its inhabitants, or a hero or champion could make his way there, with great difficulty and no guarantee of survival. It was also possible, occasionally and as a special dispensation, to request passage to the Otherworld, usually of Manannan, who might be persuaded to sail there. At certain times of the year, most notably Samhain and to a lesser extent Beltain, when the Light Year gave way to the Dark, or the Dark to the Light, the boundaries between the worlds grew thin and it was possible for an unwary mortal to stumble accidentally into the Otherworld by straying too close to one of its entrances.

This fair and blessed place did have its darker side. Time there ran at a different pace from time in the mortal world—a day in the Otherworld could equal a hundred human years. Some tales instruct the visitor to take no food or drink when a guest in Annwn, because to do so would tie one forever to the Otherworld, with no hope of return. And in some legends the "fey folk" can be casually cruel, stealing away humans as lovers or companions with no thought for their wishes or the consequences of their loss to those who were left behind.

Annwn paradoxically symbolizes both the fear of the unknown—the future, and the great unknown of what happens after death—and the belief that all will be well, that the future will be beneficial and happy, and that after our death we will still have our rebirth to look forward to, while resting and recovering in the Otherworld from the rigors of this life. It represents opposites—on the one hand stagnation and on the other disorder—and the tension between them that makes for innovation and progress.

The Wildwood

The Celtic lands were once a lush, rich wilderness of trees, a vast forest that covered much of the landscape from sea to sea. Broadleaved trees filled the land, oak and beech, ash and birch, rowan on the hills, alder and hazel, and willows at the water's edge. They provided cover, shelter, game, leaves, berries, nuts, mushrooms, herbs for medicine, and wood for fires, tools, boats, and buildings—everything the hunter-gatherer needed to survive.

As agriculture became more widespread and tribes settled down into communities, areas of land were cleared to grow crops and keep livestock, usually near rivers that could provide a plentiful supply of water. To start with, at least, they were small settlements. So small open spaces in the forest's green canopy and the wildwood still supplied much of the community's needs. But as the population increased, the need to feed people led to more and more of the great forest being cut down, until today there are only tiny patches of it left, mostly on land that can't be used for anything else. We are all by far the poorer for its loss.

We need trees, not only for their oxygen-producing, pollution-cleansing attributes, but on a more spiritual, elemental level. Trees live to an entirely different timescale from animals. Their life is measured in centuries, not years. Their needs are simple—the earth for their roots, sunlight and rain for growth, space for their spreading branches. They provide food for native animals and insects, rich compost from their fallen leaves, shelter from the weather. To the sensitive soul, there is a sense of profound awe when in the presence of an old tree, whether it's a wizened, friendly apple tree in an orchard or a massive, stoic oak in a forest.

To gain an understanding of the Celtic perception of the forest it's vital to take the time to visit a wooded area, the older the better. It must be a true wood, or forest if possible, not a plantation, and not just a few trees in a park. Go at least far enough in that you can't see any signs of human habitation or intervention, then stand for a while, stretching your senses. Tune out any sounds of traffic or aircraft. Tune in to birdsong, wind, and rustlings in the undergrowth. Be aware of how alone you are in this serenely dynamic place, which is calm and quiet yet brimming over with life. Then imagine yourself, small and delicate, in the depths of an ancient forest, the trees massive sentinels around you, their leaves obstructing your view of the sky. It's very easy to get lost in the sheer vastness surrounding you, unless you have a compass or a guide...

The Wildwood symbolizes the more primitive part of ourselves, a part of our mind we may not even recognize today. It's the part that still automatically touches wood for luck, that snarls silently when someone invades our personal space, that could kill if our life depended on it, regardless of how appalling the idea may seem in normal everyday life. It's where our survival instinct lurks. It can be a frightening place, but nevertheless it's a vitally important aspect of ourselves. Getting in touch with it, being at home with it, can be surprisingly empowering. Even simply acknowledging that we contain such a primal, untamed side can be enlightening, especially if we've always considered ourselves to be rational, civilized people.

It's important not to lose yourself. Unless you know that you can find your way, or have a guide you know you can trust, it's best to stay at the edges of the inner forest, at least to start with. Peer into the undergrowth, listen to the sounds the forest makes, learn the different scents, but don't stray too far in unless you have a path back out.

The Sea

The sea is the origin of life on earth. It covers a little over 70 percent of the world's surface, and helps drive the weather systems that contribute to keeping the planet in balance. The great sea currents carry warm water from equatorial areas to the far north and south, warming the coasts and making life possible. For the Celts, even if at the time they were unaware of what blessed their lands with warmth and prosperity, the two most important would have been the Gulf Stream and the North Atlantic current, both of which keep the UK and northern Europe temperate.

The sea was seen as both an obstacle to be overcome and a source of great riches, teeming with life. Fish, a good source of protein, probably formed a large part of the Celtic diet in coastal regions—it took a lot less energy to catch fish than to hunt a land animal. Crabs, lobsters, small crustaceans, and mollusks, such as mussels, cockles, even oysters, added variety, as did the various seaweeds growing around the coast. The Welsh delicacy laverbread is made by cooking and pulping laver seaweed (the same seaweed used by the Japanese to make nori sheets for sushi), then rolling it in oatmeal and frying in butter or pork fat. In Ireland, carrageen or Irish moss seaweed may be prepared and used as a thickener in other foods, adding to their nutritious value. It's quite possible that other types of seaweed were cooked and eaten, especially where farmed vegetables were less than abundant.

For early peoples the sea was often an impassable barrier—until boats were invented. All ancient cultures had them, for fishing in deep water if nothing else, but in Europe, where there are no particularly large stretches of open water, maritime occupations became widespread. The whole region was heavily dependent on trade, much of which was by sea, and while Celts were to a large extent self-sufficient, the British islands produced some highly desired material—Welsh gold, Cornish tin to manufacture bronze, silver, horses, and, unfortunately, slaves. In return, the inhabitants were happy to import wine, exotic foodstuffs, and luxuries.

Over time the Celts became expert mariners and boat builders—a necessary job in a world where so much depended on being able to travel safely over water, for both trade and to settle disputes by combat. The Mabinogion tells the tale of Bran taking an invasion force across the sea from Wales to Ireland to avenge the harm done to his sister by her husband, the king Matholwch. While this is a story, no doubt such raids did happen, either as revenge for slights, real or imagined, or in order to raid a rival's lands. According to Caesar's *Gallic Wars*, Celtic ships were superior to the Roman's own, built with flatter, broader hulls to allow them to navigate more easily in shallow waters, with high bows and sterns to enable them to withstand high seas. The sails were made of hides or leather, and would not tear in the vicious winds around their coasts.

The sea was more than a physical barrier or food store, however. It was also a source of profound mystery. The first non-swimmer who fell overboard from his boat soon found out that water could be deadly. Therefore, it follows, anything that can live in the sea, actually breathe underwater, must be possessed of wondrous, if not magical, abilities. The sea becomes something more than simply a body of water—it now represents a force to be respected or sometimes propitiated, its deities to be feared or asked for the blessings of their bounty.

The Otherworld was sometimes considered to be a land in the west, far across the sea towards the setting sun, to be gained only by a feat of great bravery, foolhardiness, or sacrifice. Manannan had to be persuaded to take you there in his boat—human craft were likely to sink, or be washed up on some desolate isle to act as a warning for others foolish enough to try to make the journey unaided.

For the Celts, the sea symbolized the hidden unknown and its dangers. To us, the sea symbolizes the modern concept of the unknown—the depths of the unconscious, that part of the mind that responds to subtle stimuli, the potential source of extrasensory abilities. It can be a very dangerous place, full of perils for the unwary, but at the same time vibrantly exciting. Even skimming the surface can provide new insights into ourselves, and hence others—because no matter how much we may like to think differently, we are all alike under the surface.

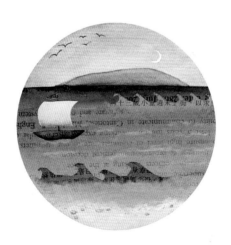

The Sacred Grove

The nymet (nemeton or sacred grove) was central to the Druid's way of life. Formed by a circle of trees on a slight rise or hillock, or at the top of a hill, the grove was church, council chamber, and court combined. Druids, and frequently the rest of the community, would gather here to worship and sacrifice, teach, pronounce judgment, arbitrate disputes, and discuss religious, tribal, and inter-tribal matters.

The ring was probably formed by removing some trees from the center of a copse, although felling trees was a serious business. All were sacred but the Great Mother would not want her children to go cold for the want of wood for building and burning. The choice of which trees to remove would be made by the Druids after much thought and prayer, and once cleared, the center would be kept clear of saplings and rough undergrowth.

The idea of the sacred grove isn't unique to the Celts. Most ancient cultures, and some modern ones, have a similar notion of a "tree-temple," and nymets can be found across the globe. Standing within one, no matter how ancient or new, gives us an extraordinary feeling of being able to reach out and touch something at once earthly and divine. There's a profound sensation of peace, safety, and groundedness, as though our own roots were stretching deep into the body of the Great Mother and finding a home there. The strange tranquility within the sacred grove soothes our fears, its roundness echoing the roundness of the womb, the world, the circle of existence. It's the shape of wholeness and infinite potential. Although the nymet has strong links with the Wildwood and its perils, at the same time there is sanctuary at the nymet's center, a familiar space where we can feel at home.

We all need sanctuary from time to time—when everything seems to be going wrong and life seems overwhelming, especially if we have others depending on us and our actions. If we can learn to carry a sacred grove within us we may alleviate at least some of that strain. Imagine a small, round, flat-topped hill, its top ringed by your favorite trees—this space is personal to you and you choose what appears here. The trees shouldn't be too close to each other and the space in the middle must be open to sky. The center can be covered with low sweet grass, or moss, or wildflowers if you prefer, but it must be clear of brambles and nettles, or anything that can hurt. Fill the encircling trees with birds if you like their song, or leave them empty if you crave silence. Give yourself something natural to sit on at the very center—an ancient moss-covered rock, perhaps, or a fallen tree-trunk. Rest for a while with your eyes closed, enjoying the peace, the sweet clean air and the scent of nature, the fragrance of growing trees and flowers. Feel the sun—or the rain, if you prefer—on your face as you raise it to the sky. Listen to the sounds around you. Feel the texture of your seat, of the ground beneath you—envision yourself barefoot to enjoy the cool moss or tickling grass. You are alone and private here. Be naked if you like, stretch and enjoy being completely yourself. Speak silently to the goddess of the grove, Nemetona. She is you and you are her while in this sacred space. Spend as long here as you can, and take back the sense of peace with you when you have to return to the external world. Your own sanctuary will be there waiting for you any time you need its gentle, powerful protection.

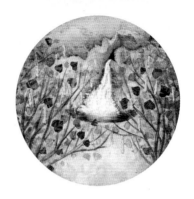

The Spring and the Ford

Natural springs of cold, clean water welling up from places underground would have been a source of wonder for the Celts, a precious gift from the Great Mother. They were often believed to have healing powers, especially if they were warm thermal springs. The water was thought to act as a carrier of knowledge from the Otherworld for those who had the wisdom to understand.

On a physical level the spring symbolizes the ability of the body to heal itself, on the mental level it's symbolic of an upwelling of inspiration and insight, while on the spiritual level it represents aspirations and a desire for improvement.

Rivers have been used as natural boundaries for as long as humans have been territorial. No one could claim to own the river between two territories—rivers were essential waterways for travel and trade, washing and fishing, watering and drinking.

Bridges were well known in ancient times but the amount of work involved in building and maintaining them made alternatives attractive. Fords—places where the river ran shallow enough for humans to walk across and drive valuable animals from one side to the other without danger—were therefore valued.

To cross a ford meant stepping from one realm to another, overcoming the obstacles on either side and walking safely through what could be a dangerous place. The ford symbolizes progress, the willingness to step beyond what is familiar into what is unknown—and a willingness to get one's feet wet in the process, to engage fully with the process of development rather than observing it from a distance.

The ford also symbolizes the reconciling of opposites, the union of two opposing forces or ideas to produce a stronger third entity, a fusion of the powers of both. It represents partnership, marriage, amalgamation, and is a potent symbol for everyone.

Labyrinth and Maze

What is generally referred to as a maze these days is actually one of two classical structures with different forms and symbolism. The original and most ancient structure is a labyrinth, usually seven-ringed, and with only one path through to the center. A maze, on the other hand, has many branching paths and sometimes more than one route, and often leads into the middle and then out again, either by the same or by different paths.

In European legend, the original labyrinth was built to confine the mythical Minotaur, a fearsome and ferocious creature, half man and half bull. The concept of the labyrinth is much older, however, possibly dating as far back as 2,500 BCE. It seems that most labyrinths were open to the air, their walls marked by stones in northern Europe. In the UK and some areas of central Europe they were turf-walled.

A number of purposes have been suggested for the labyrinth. The fact it was used in legend as a trap for a malevolent monster suggests that others may have been used for a similar purpose, perhaps to capture malicious spirits. Mosaic labyrinths on the floors near the doorways of Roman dwellings may have served a symbolic protective purpose, confounding the entrance of evil. The pattern was also used for the Lusus Trojae, in which the labyrinth was navigated on horseback. However, as far as the majority of Celts were concerned, it's more likely that the labyrinth served as a form of ritual for dance, or for what today would be called meditation.

Walking the labyrinth produces a stillness of mind and spirit. The concentration needed to follow the path correctly, especially if it was constructed around a hill like that of Glastonbury Tor (see page 135), focused the mind and the senses. The outside world receded as the inner consciousness took over. You could feel you were walking with the gods, silently communing with the spirits of the place, venerating the Great Mother. At the center of the labyrinth you would pause, mind refreshed and spirits raised, in quiet celebration of life and all it can give. If the center of the labyrinth was at the top of a hill, you would be able to look out over the land and find contentment in the view, in the familiar shape of the country seen from a different perspective. Gazing at the rich and subtle blue of the sky above, and the green and fertile land below, resting at the heart of the labyrinth allows a glimpse of the infinite. It's no surprise that the shape of the labyrinth resembles the human brain, even if it was probably a happy accident. Following the labyrinth symbolically unites the two halves of the mind to create a harmonious whole.

Dancing along the paths, while more energetic than walking, has a similar effect, soothing the active part of the being while energizing the passive, contemplative self. Following the labyrinth is nevertheless a joyous celebration of unity with one's family and friends, the community and the land on which we all live.

The maze, however, is designed as a challenge. It's a test of memory and practical skills. You have to use all your senses to find your way safely and swiftly through. It's also occasionally a test of balance, depending on the structure of the maze. Modern-day paper mazes and mental puzzles perform the same function but on a more cerebral level. There's a certain sense of danger in treading even the simplest maze—you can never know who or what lurks around the next corner. Then there is relief and a sense of satisfaction on a safe and successful exit.

In today's world, the labyrinth symbolizes an inward journey, contemplation, and the absence of strong emotion. It's a symbol of the stillness we all need from time to time, simply to let our minds and imaginations rest and recoup from everyday stress. The maze is symbolic of our day-to-day life, and how we have to negotiate our way through problems and choices in order to survive. In general terms, both represent the things we have to do alone, without help from anyone else.

The Roundhouse

Celtic families lived in roundhouses constructed from a ring of upright posts with walls of thin flexible hazel or willow sticks (wattle) interlaced between them. These were coated with daub and the whole covered by a pitched thatched roof. The larger roundhouses had a second ring of uprights to help support the rafters that carried the weight of the roof. The basic design of the building had no windows and only one doorway, which faced south and east to take best advantage of the available sunlight. Grander buildings, those owned by the king or chief, might also have a small "porch" added outside the door. While the daub—a mixture of clay to bind, earth, straw, or crushed chalk for bulk, and straw or hair to provide strength and flexibility—was still damp, it would be covered with lime plaster to make it waterproof and to seal any cracks, and the inner wall and supporting upright posts would be painted with a lime wash, and possibly in colorful patterns. This was to brighten the interior since the only light entering the building came through the doorway, or was provided by the central fire.

The materials used in construction were freely available and abundant, but the walls were prone to cracking and dampness, given their flexibility and the rigors of the weather, and the thatch needed patching and replacing regularly. Keeping the roundhouse repaired and weatherproof would have been an important job.

It's likely that there was no hole for the smoke from the central fire to escape, as that would have let in the rain. Instead it would have made its way through the thatch, which could be a little dangerous if the thatch was completely dry. However, this system also served a useful purpose. Smoking meat and fish hung up on the rafters over the fire was a good way of preserving food. It was also useful for drying herbs for cooking and medicinal use.

The beds, arranged together by one part of the wall, were usually made of a sturdy wooden frame, probably oak, with a straw or feather mattress supported by springy woven hazel sticks. It seems likely that the working area ranged along the opposite side of the circle and included a quern for grinding grain for bread, perhaps a bread oven in the larger families, a loom, a place for tools, and possibly a lathe if the family was wealthy enough. Wooden buckets and tubs, bowls, mugs, spoons, and ladles were used as well as fired clay pottery for food, cooking, and water storage. The family collected vegetables and wild nuts and berries in wickerwork baskets. Individual possessions, jewelry, and spare clothing were kept in chests or on display – display of one's wealth and therefore status was an innate part of Celtic life.

Life in the roundhouse was cozy and relatively comfortable. The floors would be covered with sheepskin and leather hides to keep out the cold and damp, there would be stools for seating and at least one low table for eating, and while the lack of light and smokiness from the fire might make it gloomy on rainy days, the constant companionship meant that no one would ever be lonely or in need.

The Celts knew of square and rectangular buildings but far preferred their own roundhouses, perhaps because of the intimacy and natural shape. They symbolize safety, the womb, the protection of the Mother Goddess, and the vital family connections that keep society going.

The Field and the Farm

Celtic society was primarily agrarian. Each small community, or possibly family in the larger settlements, would have a patchwork of individual fields in which to grow cereal crops and vegetables. In Britain these included beans, fat hen—now considered a weed, but high in vitamin C and eaten as greens in ancient times—wild carrots, and a native ancestor of the parsnip. In the warmer climes of northern Europe, a wider variety of vegetables were grown, including onions and leeks, and many kinds of fruit. Cereal crops included oats, rye, millet, and barley, and later spelt and emmer wheat. The fields were considerably smaller than today's vast acreages, and were square or rectangular because these were the easiest shapes to plough. Fields were worked with an iron plough, usually pulled by oxen. Corn in all its varieties was sufficiently important to the Celts to appear on their coinage. It constituted a large part of the diet in the form of breads, and was added to stews and brewed to produce ales.

Animals were important to the Celtic way of life. Wealth was perceived as the number of cattle an individual owned, and cows and bulls had their parts to play—cows to give milk and bulls to pull ploughs (see page 96). Celtic sheep were rougher and hardier than the sheep with which we're familiar today, and were kept mainly for their milk and wool. They were killed and the mutton eaten when they reached the end of their useful lives.

The Celts also kept a variety of domestic pig, goats, chickens, and geese, although if Julius Caesar is to be believed, the Celts did not actually eat chickens or geese. Chickens were kept for their eggs but geese were considered a symbol of aggressive guardianship and may have been used to warn of danger or scare off small predators. Continental Celts associated them particularly with Roman-adopted war-gods and occasionally wore their image as a helmet crest.

Pigs, goats, and poultry could be kept close to the homestead, but sheep and cattle require more grazing space and were prevalent among upland communities. Even there they were brought down from the pastures to spend the winter in enclosures outside the village—or possibly inside their own separate roundhouses, which served as barns, protecting the herd from the weather and from predators.

The field symbolizes self-sufficiency and self-reliance. It also represents hard work and communal labor. Everyone was expected to pull together to provide for the clan, unless prevented by youth, age, or ill-health.

CELTIC COIN
WITH CORN

The Hillfort

The basic Celtic fort was composed simply of a settlement surrounded by a deep ditch, the earth from which was piled up into a bank on the inner side. Anyone trying to attack was faced with a very steep climb up a high bank of pounded earth, and usually people on the top throwing rocks, dung, or other less savory things down on their heads. Such a structure could be built by any community, whether they lived on a hill or in a valley.

Hillforts, however, were much more imposing dwelling places. As the name implies, they were generally built on the tops of hills, and could be huge, holding an entire community of tens of large roundhouses and hundreds of people, and their livestock, keeping them safe behind its many bank and ditch fortifications.

The hillfort symbolizes the security of the walled city, the gated community, the ability to shut out the world and keep danger at bay. It carries with it the risk of cutting yourself off from the rest of the world, and while that may be appealing, it's not the best way to engage with life. There are times, however, when it's the only way to survive. The skill lies in deciding when to retrench, and when to tackle the enemy head on.

The Cromlech and the Cave

Many ancient lands are dotted with what appear to be large stone tables, usually three upright slabs supporting a flattish stone on top. These are known as cromlechs or quoits in Wales and Cornwall, the last bastions of Celtic culture in mainland UK, or more generally as dolmen, from the Breton for "stone table." These were the tombs of important people, and would originally have been covered with earth, gradually revealing their inner structure as the soil was washed or blown away. They predate the Celts by several thousand years, but were such a startling feature of the landscape that they quickly acquired a magical and mystical significance.

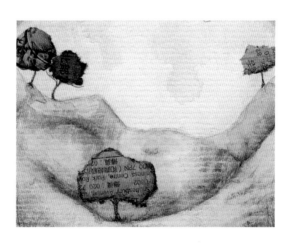

Caves were deemed to be entrances into the body of the Great Mother, giving access to her secrets and the hidden knowledge contained within her. They symbolized her womb. They provided shelter, too, on occasion, much as a mother would protect her children from the weather or from unfriendly eyes. Springs often flowed from caves, bringing the knowledge and wisdom of the Otherworld up to the surface to be shared by all who chose to drink of the waters, or to be used to heal the sick and suffering.

Both the cromlech and the cave were entrances to Annwn, and were treated with great respect. They symbolize unrealized potential, innate and latent talents, the possibilities hidden within the human body and mind. Symbolically, they can most easily be accessed in dreams, and keeping a record of our dreams, and analysing them, can be one of the most effective ways of exploring our inner selves. It is plausible that the Celts perceived dreaming as the essence of the self leaving the physical body at night, and that spirit or soul was the part of the being that traveled to the Otherworld to await its rebirth—hence the spirit could gain knowledge of the Otherworld in its nightly wanderings.

It certainly does no harm to try! Our dreams are intimate reflections of our minds and the ways they work, and properly understood can be immensely revealing.

Conclusion

Celtic Twilight

Celtic culture flourished for almost three thousand years across Europe and the British Isles, until the Romans began to expand their empire, gradually and relentlessly forcing most of Europe into submission. Eventually much of Britain was overcome. The Druid university on the Island of Mona—modern-day Anglesey in Wales—was destroyed in the Emperor Claudius's invasion of 43 BCE, and it was after this that Boudica took her own life. The bond with the Great Mother continued, however, and in Ireland, Wales, and the Cornish tip of England, where the Romans never gained a foothold, the culture endured for some centuries, until the establishment of the Christian faith during the fifth and sixth centuries CE.

Initially, the new faith was welcomed. What was one more god among so many? The Christian monks were decent enough fellows, adopting Celtic art forms and fashioning them into bibles and crosses to adorn their buildings. It was a vibrant, mystical faith. Everything in life and nature expressed the Christian god's glorious creation of the world and all that was in it—which accorded well with the Celtic view of the land as the sacred body of the Great Mother. As time went on, though, the interpreted teachings of Paul and the fledgling Catholic church began to infiltrate the faith, teaching that the human body and its desires were sinful and should be punished, that the world had been created for man's use and dominion, and that instead of a unified vision of the harmony of all things the world should be seen in terms of good and evil—mostly evil. With sound political sense—since they could not simply force the populace to worship the Christian god—Christianity took over the ancient sacred places and built churches on them, relegated the Celtic deities to saints where they could and evil spirits where they could not, and changed that

quintessential figure of the Celtic spirit, Cernunnos, into the devil. What millennia of warfare could not accomplish was achieved in a matter of centuries by a repressive religion.

From around the tenth century CE the Celtic culture was all but forgotten until the age of Queen Victoria, when a sudden upsurge in interest in all things ancient brought the Celts to the attention of a population searching for a national identity and relief from the grimness of the Industrial Revolution. Since then, archaeologists and anthropologists have been uncovering facts about these dynamic people.

We have no magnificent temples to admire—the land itself was their temple. They did not institute any enduring systems of government, politics, military, or academia—once the Druids were gone there was no one to carry the ancient knowledge. They had no interest in empire building, content to keep to their patchwork of independent tribes and tribal leaders. Some of their legends, songs, and tales remain, handed down through the ages, and notable for their robust, exciting subjects and style. Their metalwork, and especially their jewelry, remain an inspiration. And in these times their understanding of the connections between the land and everything that depends upon it—every living thing upon its face, in its oceans, or on the wing above the earth—is a lesson to us all. We cannot live without the generosity of the earth, the ultimate Great Mother. If we wish to survive, it's past time to treat her with the reverence she deserves, and do what we can to reverse the damage we have caused.

Index